MILLENNIUM BILTMORE

A Grand Hotel Born of Hollywood Dreams

Ward Morehouse III

Published by BearManor Media
New York, New York
2014

For Katherine Boynton

Millennium Biltmore
Copyright © 2013 by Ward Morehouse III.
All Rights Reserved.
ISBN 978-1-59393-748-2

No part of this book may be reproduced in any form or by any means, electronic, mechanical, digital, photocopying or recording, except for the inclusion in a review, without permission in writing from the publisher.

Published in the USA by:
BearManor Media
PO Box 1129
Duncan, Oklahoma 73534-1129
www.bearmanormedia.com

Printed in the United States of America
Front cover, back cover, pages 93, and 94 photographs courtesy of Sam Dyees
All other photographs courtesy of the Millennium Biltmore
Book design by Bob Antler, Antler Designworks

The Millennium Biltmore Hotel, Millennium & Copthorne Hotels, plc, and its affiliates and their respective directors, officers, and employees, make no representation or warranties with respect to the accuracy, applicability, fitness, or completeness of the contents of this publication. The statements, views and opinions contained in the book are entirely those of the author, and shall not be attributable to the Millennium Biltmore Hotel, Millennium & Copthorne Hotels, plc, and its affiliates and their respective directors, officers, and employees.

Preface

I have been very fortunate in my life to have had access to many of the world's finest hotels. As a writer who specializes in chronicling the splendors of these fabled institutions, I not only get to sleep in the gorgeous, lush beds, I not only am treated to the finest cuisine whipped up by the world's greatest chefs in some of the globe's most splendid dining spaces, but, unlike even the most cherished and richest of their guests, I get a first-hand, behind-the-scenes tour of these modern-day pleasure palaces, usually conducted by no less than the hotel's general manager.

Frankly, I have over the years become rather spoiled. But no matter how many great hotels I am privileged to stay at, no matter how many fine chocolates are laid upon my satin pillow cover as evening falls, I'm never tired of the sheer grandiosity of these great buildings. Because, though they may seem to be rather similar to the casual observer, and yes though they do tend to share many traits, such as great service and attention to details, they are all, when all is said and done, quite unique.

This point was driven home yet again when I came out to Los Angeles to begin my exploration of the great Millennium Biltmore. Once again, there was excitement in the hotel air for me as I took that first step into the deep, plush nap of its carpets. Because a great hotel exerts a great influence on the great city it usually dwells in. The Waldorf Astoria and the Plaza, different as they are, both have left their impression on the island of Manhattan, just as the world of New York deeply influences both of those great institutions. The same is true of the Ritz and the Savoy in London, both quite different establishments, but both as much a part of the great history of London as two resplendent jewels set in the English crown on display at the Tower.

Rendezvous Court, originally the hotel lobby

Los Angeles and the Millennium Biltmore immediately hit me as yet another unique and marvelous combination of urban environment and grand hotel. The vibe, if you will, of L.A. is really quite different from any other American city. The closest I can come to describing it is as if Paris were situated on the Côte d'Azur. A great metropolis plunked down where one usually finds a great resort town. L.A. has the best of both. A financial district and world-class beaches.

The movie industry, the dream factory, also exudes its great influence on both hotel and city. Los Angeles is more of a one-industry town than most great metropolises. But what an industry! And what denizens it boasts! The best and the brightest, the most ambitious and the most beautiful have been pouring into this city for a hundred years now. It shows in the gene pool. Even the people who aren't movie stars often look like movie stars.

I suppose we all have Thomas Edison to thank for Tinsel Town. It was his somewhat rapacious attempt to corner the movie industry market back in New York that forced his competitors to take their cameras to some locale where the Wizard of Menlo Park couldn't reach them. That meant the exact opposite coast. Legend has it that they picked Hollywood simply because it was the last stop on the train and they could travel no farther west from New York. And, of course, it had great weather, at a time when all moviemaking was an outdoor affair, even the interior shots.

Well, the movie industry did pretty well for itself in Southern California, which up until that time had been a rather sleepy farming community, producing mostly oranges. With prosperity comes growth and

Crystal Ballroom

with growth comes tourists and businessmen looking for fine accommodations. The Millennium Biltmore was the first fine hotel erected to cater to these folks in Los Angeles. The movie industry, at last check, is still a going concern and so is that great lady of L.A., the Millennium Biltmore.

Here I would like to thank the late Norman Simpson, author of *Country Inns and Back Roads*, who helped lead the way for me to write books on hotels. My philosophy: "I have come to realize that it is a book written for people who like to read as well as go to inns," Simpson said. "I look for a distinct personal involvement with guests between the innkeepers and their staff." Obviously, there is a difference with a grand hotel. The staff cannot be expected to give the personal details of guests' lives, with some exceptions. But the Millennium Biltmore prides itself on having what guests want at the hotel, down to the very rooms they had last time, and even what they often ordered from room service. They are treated like family members.

Contents

Preface...5

Biltmore Chronology...11

Introduction...19

1	An Arabian Night's Dream of a Hotel	25
2	Adding to Prosperity: The Biltmore Addition	47
3	The Biltmore Theatre	57
4	It Happened Many Nights: The Oscars at the Biltmore	63
5	Thelma Becker, Queen of the Biltmore, and Other Stars at the Hotel	75
6	Service at the Biltmore	89
7	Chairman Kwek, the Globe-Trekking Businessman Bringing the Biltmore into the Third Millennum	97
8	Pershing Square and the Movie Palaces	107

9   Zeppelin (Graf not Led) Stops at the
Millennium Biltmore   113

10   The Black Dahlia and the 1960 Democratic
Convention—Furtive Doings at the Biltmore   117

11   Other Grand Los Angeles Hotels   127

Check Out...141

Appendix A:
Movies, and Other Things, Shot at the Biltmore...143

Appendix B:
My Father's Exclusive Interviews
with Some Hollywood Heavyweights...163

Appendix C:
My Stepmother, the Bon Vivant...171

Appendix D:
Chicago Newspaperman Joe Hyams Goes Hollywood...179

Appendix E:
Valentino Writes!...183

Appendix F:
Damon Runyon Marvels at the Biltmore's own
"Guys and Dolls"...189

Biltmore Chronology

The hotel has experienced some remarkable events throughout the past century:

1921
City boosters form the Central Investment Corp. to finance construction of a hotel that would be a symbol of Los Angeles' success and ambition.

1922
Architects Schultze & Weaver complete the design and excavation begins. The building is finished in a record-breaking 18 months at a cost of approximately, $10 million.

1923
Hotel opens October 1 as the largest hotel west of Chicago. Over 3,000 guests attend the Gala opening and dinner, including Cecil B. DeMille.

1924
Humorist Will Rogers emcees the opening of the Biltmore Theatre, while Schultze & Weaver return to begin a $4 million expansion.

1927
The Academy of Motion Picture Arts & Sciences is founded at a banquet in the Crystal Ballroom. Legend says the Oscar statue was sketched here on a Biltmore napkin.

October 1, 1923 opening night gala

1929

Germany's Graf Zeppelin soars over the hotel on a round-the-world trip sponsored by newspaper magnate William Randolph Hearst. The Biltmore kitchen replenishes the dirigible's commissary.

1931

Fourth Annual Academy Awards are held November 10 in the Sala d'Oro ballroom.

1933

Hotelier Baron Long takes control of the hotel during the Great Depression and transforms the Sala d'Oro into the world's largest nightclub, the Biltmore Bowl, which opens to the big band sounds of Jimmy Grier and Harry James.

1935–39; 1941–43

The Biltmore hosts the Academy Awards.

Academy Awards 1937. Mega-producer Cecil B. DeMille facing left, lower left, and Henry Fonda front center facing left

1942

The hotel becomes a military rest and recreation facility during World War II.

1947

Actress Elizabeth Short, the "Black Dahlia," is last seen alive in the lobby before her still-unexplained death.

1950

A small fire destroys part of the Biltmore Bowl, and during remodeling, the floor is raised to create the Regency Room beneath.

1960
The Music Room (now the lobby) serves as campaign headquarters for John F. Kennedy during the 1960 Democratic National Convention. Running mate Lyndon Johnson is based in the Emerald Room.

1967
The Biltmore Theatre closes its doors with the opening of the Los Angeles Music Center.

1969
The Cultural Heritage Board of L.A. designates the hotel an Historic Monument.

1977

The Academy of Motion Picture Arts & Sciences celebrates the 50th anniversary of Oscar with a party in the Crystal Ballroom hosted by Bob Hope.

1980

The Biltmore is awarded the prestigious National Honor Award from the American Institute of Architects.

1981

President Ronald Reagan is fêted at a farewell luncheon before moving into the White House.

1984

The Biltmore serves as headquarters for the International Olympic Committee during the 1984 games in Los Angeles. The same year, the hotel undergoes a massive $135 million renovation that moves the lobby from the Rendezvous Court to the Music Room.

1987

Renovation is completed and includes the addition of the Biltmore Tower office structure, extensive mural restoration by one of the original decorators' sons, and the creation of the Gallery Bar from a corridor door leading to Grand Ave.

1988

The Hotel is the site for a Royal Gala honoring the Duke and Duchess of York in the Crystal Ballroom.

1999

The Biltmore becomes the first hotel in Los Angeles to enact a "Green Policy," encouraging guests to reuse their linens to conserve energy.

2000
Hotel acquired by Millennium Hotels & Resorts.

2008
The Hotel celebrates its 85th Anniversary with a gala celebration and a certificate from the City of Los Angeles.

2011
Serving as an iconic filming location for decades, the Biltmore hosts 52 filming, video and photography projects in one year, averaging one a week.

2013
The landmark Hotel celebrates its 90th Anniversary, featuring 683 guestrooms and 70,000 square feet of architecturally grand meeting and banquet space.

In the fourth quarter, the hotel introduces a new Singaporean-Chinese casual restaurant called Bugis Street Brasserie: the first in the U.S. and fifth globally within Millennium & Copthorne Hotels.

Introduction

"When I first got to L.A., I used to walk up and down the corridors of the Millennium Biltmore to soak up the atmosphere and glamour of Hollywood," RKO Pictures chairman, Broadway producer and former actor Ted Hartley said in an interview for this book. Hartley is married to actress Dina Merrill.

The early owners of the Millennium Biltmore brought an unfailing devotion to the art of hotel keeping as well as an unparalleled elegance to a competitive, highly profitable business. Not only did the Millennium Biltmore become the grandest of them all on the West Coast, but significantly influenced the building of other L.A. grand hotels. It set the standard, even to this day, by which other hotels were built and judged, much the same as the original Waldorf Astoria did in 1893.

In a larger sense, Los Angeles can be divided into two eras, before and after the Millennium Biltmore. Before, it was much like New York, that is, New York before the advent of the Waldorf Astoria's opening in 1893. All of a sudden, London or Paris didn't tower figuratively over New York's hotel life. So, too, with the Millennium Biltmore. The Millennium Biltmore opened in 1923 to national acclaim as the largest hotel west of Chicago, and by 1969, was designated a Historic Cultural Landmark by the City of Los Angeles.

Originally, the idea for the hotel arose out of a desire to create a grand icon to show the rest of the country that Los Angeles had "arrived." By 1920, filmmaking was Los Angeles's biggest industry and the perfect climate its biggest attraction. But the city had no landmark hotel until a prominent banker named Joseph Sartori called a meeting of forty of the city's business leaders to suggest building one. The group persuaded hotelier John McEntee Bowman to finance the project, and named it "The Biltmore" after other hotels in the country he had developed. Today, "Biltmore" hotels are unrelated except in name.

In just 47 days, New York architectural firm Schultze and Weaver came up with the $10 million design. A Beaux Arts composition, with Spanish-Italian Renaissance detail, was meant as a throwback to the Castilian heritage of the city. And the angel theme throughout the hotel is a symbol of the city as well as the hotel itself.

"Schultze & Weaver (who went on to design The Breakers in Palm Beach and the Waldorf Astoria in New York) were not only design makers of the century, they are representative of the triumph of the Industrial Revolution," Joseph Caponnetto, who became director of the Schultze & Weaver/Lloyd Morgan Architectural Archive, told me for my book *The Waldorf Astoria: America's Gilded Dream*. The Millennium Biltmore gave guests the feeling that they experienced some of Italy's grandest designs in Southern California, just as The Breakers and Waldorf Astoria helped transport their guests to worlds far afield from the beautiful but boring beaches of Florida and the jangling hustle and bustle of New York City.

The Biltmore in Los Angeles was completed in just 18 months and opened October 1, 1923 to a weeklong celebration featuring a gala attended by Cecil B. DeMille, Jack Warner and Mary Pickford with seven orchestras in eight dining rooms. The brand new grand hotel boasted 916 guestrooms and 826 bathrooms on 11 floors. In 1927, 500 more rooms were added. An instant triumph, the hotel's flawless service standards and luxurious appointments made it the premier West Coast destination. The 1700-seat Biltmore Theatre was constructed in 1924, on the corner of Grand Avenue, attached to the hotel—it ran sold-out plays continuously until it was closed in the mid-1960s, when the Dorothy Chandler Pavilion and Music Center opened nearby. Lucille Ball, Mae West, and the world-famous acting couple Alfred Lunt and Lynn Fontanne graced the stage of the Biltmore Theatre, along with many others.

Throughout the years, the hotel has undergone several restorations, notably a $30 million renovation in the mid-1970s and a $135 million project between 1984 and 1987, when the main lobby was relocated from its original location in the Rendezvous Court (to accompany the new valet entrance). Two floors of rooms were converted into offices (now storage and maintenance), murals were touched up, walls repainted and the marble fountain was added to the Rendezvous Court. Today, the hotel is owned by Millennium Hotels and Resorts and joins a family of fifteen properties in North America, as well as more than 100 hotels globally.

"Without a doubt, it's the finest hotel in the world," said *World Traveler* magazine in its October 1923 edition.

"A hotel so grand. It gets compliments everywhere in the world," the *Los Angeles Times* said in its tribute story to the hotel on its 75th anniversary in 1998.

If Palm Beach is considered the world's winter playground, I like to think of L.A. as America's Riviera. And like Palm Beach, gone are the days when downtown L.A. closed at 10 pm.

"Working with a hotel like this is one-of-a-kind. Every day you develop a real affinity to the hotel," explains Wanda Chan, the current general manager. "I feel the staff here has the same passion about this hotel—a love that you can't really describe in words. Everyone, I can say, is very proud to be part of this hotel and feels humbled to be part of its history."

"Eleven thousand people—society, business and the movie industry—clamored for tickets to the October 2 opening-night gala, but only 3,000 were invited to feast in eight dining rooms to the accompaniment of seven orchestras and hundreds of trilling red canaries," the *Los Angeles Times* said in 1995. "Celebrants marveled at the hotel's Spanish-Italian Renaissance decor, the lobby sweeping double staircase, the intricately painted ceilings, the elaborate touches in wood and bronze and glass everywhere.

"But the hit of the evening was fashion doyenne Peggy Hamilton, who arrived dressed in a floor-length white silk dress painted to resemble the Crystal Ballroom's ceiling, crafted by Vatican artist Giovanni

Peggy Hamilton in Biltmore dress

Smeraldi. Deep pockets in the skirt fanned out like the room's private dining balconies. And in her blonde hair, Hamilton wore tiny replicas of the ballroom's massive crystal chandeliers.

"Lou Ahern, 78, of West Hills remembers those glamour days. She was just three years old and a star of the Our Gang movies in 1923 when she became the child model in the hotel's fashion shows that featured actresses Colleen Moore, Clara Bow, Vilma Banky, Marion Davies, and others.

Introduction

"The Academy of Motion Picture Arts & Sciences was officially formed in 1927 in the Millennium Biltmore's Crystal Ballroom, and that Oscar—the movie industry's "golden boy"—was born there as a pencil sketch on a linen napkin. Then-Senator John F. Kennedy took over the hotel's Music Room (now the lobby) as his headquarters during the 1960 Democratic National Convention."

"I've worked in the hospitality industry in the greater L.A. area for more than 20 years—from Beverly Hills to the beach, and from the airport area to downtown, and I can say without a doubt that the greatest privilege has been working for an iconic hotel like the Biltmore," says Tommy Chow, director of sales and marketing for the landmark property. "Quite simply, there is no other hotel like the historic Biltmore in L.A., which makes it such a rewarding experience to work with clients whose events, meetings or filming on location are unparalleled thanks to the unforgettable grand features of its ballrooms and public spaces, and the impeccable service our staff provides at every opportunity."

"No day is the same," says David Romano, the hotel's director of catering, "and it's always incredibly colorful, from the President arriving to the Duchess of York. And catering 50-70 glorious weddings annually in our unforgettable venues, our catering and banquet teams' jobs could not be more rewarding. In fact, the rewards are directly proportional to the pressure. A couple's wedding day is among the most important in their lives, so we need to get every detail right. And when the event of a lifetime comes off without a glitch, we know we've fulfilled our role to deliver a dream-come-true occasion."

But the grand old hotel is not just a playground for the rich and famous. Office workers from the nearby jewelry district bring sack lunches and discreetly dine for free in the splendor of the Rendezvous Court, the ornate old lobby; nobody ever asks them to leave. During much of the year, the former lobby is also the place for an elegant afternoon tea at affordable prices. And three or four weddings are booked into the hotel's fancy ballrooms each weekend.

When I interviewed Chairman Kwek, (whose full name and business title, by the way, is Kwek Leng Beng, Chairman, Millennium & Copthorne, plc) in London in 2007 it was before he built the St. Regis in Singapore. And even then he was talking about the synergistic effect of the arts in hotels. It's a strategy that I came to appreciate all the more as I sat in the Gallery Bar of the Millennium Biltmore.

As an author who has written books on the Plaza Hotel, the Waldorf Astoria, and many of London's great hotels, I was completely unprepared by the architectural grandeur, legendary Hollywood-Tinsel Town sheer theatrical glamour of the Millennium Biltmore, until staying there when it all became clear. While I was still unprepared for the world-class service, it was like I was a child again, running through the corridor door of the Plaza Hotel on the way to my father's Suite 600-661.

Like being in the movie *Citizen Kane*, about a fictional newspaper czar, where everything was superhumanly grand. Not only as a child of six or eight, but an adult who'd stayed in some of the world's greatest hotels. Staying there even reminded me of my father Ward Morehouse, who wrote the "Broadway After Dark" column (second only to Winchell in publicity clout for many years) for the old *New York Sun*, and wrote several movies in the 1930s, including *Gentlemen of the Press*. Dad when he was in L.A. stayed at the now vacated Garden of Allah on Sunset Boulevard, but he went to parties at the Millennium Biltmore—and what parties they were!

Sometimes I think of the Millennium Biltmore as a beautiful film star of yesteryear. Hedy Lamarr, Jean Harlow come to mind. A real bombshell of a hotel. Of today's film stars, Jennifer Garner comes to mind, as she often does, though of course she's now married to actor Ben Affleck. Or maybe Michelle Pfeiffer, who sang her heart out in the Crystal Ballroom starring in *The Fabulous Baker Boys*. A glamorous, classy blond. The kind in which old Hollywood seemed at times to be knee-deep. So switch on the lights, the camera, and the action, as here's the hotel that has seen hundreds of movies, TV shows and commercials shot within its storied walls, and now has laid out the red carpet for you, dear reader.

1

An Arabian Night's Dream of a Hotel

Long before construction of the Millennium Biltmore, proclaimed as a "monument to the growth and prosperity of the city," could begin it had to be designed. And on December 17, 1921, architects-designers Schultze and Weaver began what the media of the time called "one of the brightest stars in the firmament of local enterprise." It certainly promised to be and did become the largest construction project in the history of Los Angeles up to that time.

Influenced heavily by Italian and Spanish Renaissance architecture, the architectural firm of Schultze and Weaver blueprinted the hotel in just 47 days. The partnership of Leonard Schultze and S. Fullerton Weaver would later leave indelible work in New York with the Waldorf Astoria in 1931, and also on other grand Gotham projects.

The Millennium Biltmore was the firm's first major commission, but had the blessing of John McEntee Bowman, a Canadian-born hotelier who was the founding president of Bowman-Biltmore Hotel, built in New York in 1913. Bowman, who had silent movie star good looks himself was coming into one of the leading hotel names in the world.

What's in a name? In 1923, the name "Biltmore" was magic. And no one knew this better than John Bowman who headed a syndicate that included the Ansonia, Commodore and Biltmore Hotels. And one of the Vanderbilts persuaded Bowman to name the new Los Angeles hotel after the Biltmore hotels and George Vanderbilt's chateau in Ashville,

Just before start of construction on largest construction project in LA history up to that time

North Carolina. But, first, Bowman had to be persuaded to head up a hotel in an area that many felt was still a kind of wild west compared to the more gentile and cultured San Francisco. In fact the Central Investment Committee even dispatched a committee to lobby for the project.

Excavation began on March 27, 1922. For the next 30 days, three steam shovels and 50 trucks ran day and night, including Sundays, to remove more than 76,000 cubic yards of earth. According to the 2003 book, *The Los Angeles Biltmore: Host of the Coast* by Margaret Leslie Davis, "approximately 5300 tons of rock and gravel, requiring 8000 truckloads and 46,000 barrels of cement were then used to lay the immense foundation.

"The building's framework, consisting of 5200 tons of fabricated steel furnished by the Well and Ironworks of Los Angeles, was completed in less than five months under the watchful eyes of E. E. M. Scofield of the Scofield Engineering-Construction Company. Nearly 1.5 million feet of lumber was delivered to the site in 374 truckloads. The Millennium Biltmore's advanced electrical system required the largest electrical permit issued in the history of Los Angeles—for more than 125 miles of wire, almost the distance from Los Angeles to San Diego.

"Schultze and Weaver had set the completion date for December 1, 1923, but the entire project was finished in an astounding 18 months, two months ahead of schedule. In addition, it was completed under budget for less than the projected $10 million total."

"There were two major ballrooms when the hotel opened in 1923—one was the Music Room now our lobby; the other was the Grand Ballroom, now our Crystal Ballroom. The Millennium Biltmore seems to have consistent features that give it a sense of place; there was a Palm

Steel girders of Biltmore rising

Room in all the Biltmore hotels; there was a dining room in all the Biltmore hotels." So says Steve Eberhard, banquet maître d' for the Millennium Biltmore.

Taking a tour of this landmark hotel, let's start with Rendezvous Court, which was the original lobby of the hotel designed by Giovanni Smeraldi. The walls are made of Italian travertine stone and the three-story ceiling is Moorish plaster with hand-painted beams, carved wood and 24-carat gold accents. Both bronze and crystal chandeliers were imported from Italy in 1923; the fountain was added in 1986 and is made of Tennessee Rose marble.

A member of The Los Angeles Cultural Heritage Board said of Smeraldi's work at the Millennium Biltmore that "the excellence of Smeraldi's masterpieces enables the Biltmore to possess an elegance found only in the palaces and public buildings of Italy, Spain and France." There's also a rather famous public building in Washington, D.C. in which his work was showcased at least to a small extent: The White House.

You'll see quite a mixture of themes in the hotel's artwork—cherubs and rams at the end of each ceiling impost, shields with coats of arms of noble Spanish conquistador families and figures of mythological creatures called griffins (also seen at the bottom of the staircase railings). The grand bronze doorway here is designed in the Spanish Baroque style, with an astrological clock installed in 1923 that still keeps time today. You'll see two figures on the stairwell front—on the left is the Roman goddess of agriculture, Ceres, and on the right is the Spanish conquistador Balboa. And of course, the angel appears in various forms throughout the hotel.

Traditional Afternoon Tea is served here Wednesday through Sunday, as well as cocktails, coffee, pastries and fruit at the Café Rendezvous, plus light meals from a limited menu in the afternoon daily. This space is one of the most photographed and filmed spots in the hotel, having been seen in films like *Daredevil*, *The Nutty Professor* and *Beverly Hills Cop* and TV series *Without a Trace*, *Mad Men*, *Glee* and *Heroes*, to name a few.

It's here also where Steve Eberhard interviews propective employees. Their interviews here are meant to convey some of the high degree

An Arabian Night's Dream of a Hotel 29

of hospitality and warmth with which the hotel expects its employees to treat its guests.

The lobby itself was originally the Music Room (and Rendezvous Court was the Lobby), where fashionable tea dances were held in the early 1930s. These dances were so popular they spilled out into the

Original first floor plan

Galeria Ceiling

Galeria and eventually into the Gold Room across the way. It didn't become the main lobby until after the 1984 renovation, when the walkways in and out of the Galeria were opened up to allow the room to function more efficiently.

The walls were once covered in a series of soft tapestries, but the travertine and oak paneling is original. The current mural behind the front desk, which was created for the hotel by a firm called Acme Fine Arts, depicts a 19th century garden with the Los Angeles skyline behind it that includes images of the Central Library and City Hall. It was

An Arabian Night's Dream of a Hotel

ABOVE: Main Lobby
BELOW: Rendezvous Court

taken down after it was damaged in a 1994 earthquake and put back up after restoration by a former concierge of the hotel.

The marble fountain is original and still spouts. The inlaid carpet mimics the pattern of the ceiling and artificial skylight. The lobby was featured in the original *Ghostbusters* film.

The Music Room also once served as the election headquarters for John F. Kennedy during the Democratic National Convention, held in Los Angeles in 1960; the Millennium Biltmore served as the headquarters hotel. His running mate (and former rival) Lyndon B. Johnson was set up across the Galeria in the Emerald Room, while the third contender, Adlai Stevenson, was set up in the space now known as the Gold Room.

Moving from the Lobby, we come to the Gallery Bar and Cognac Room. The Gallery Bar is actually NOT the hotel's original bar—when the hotel was built the space was a corridor leading to Grand Avenue, and was only recently enclosed and designed to match the decor of

The Galeria

An Arabian Night's Dream of a Hotel

The original Music Room is now the Biltmore's lobby.

the rest of the hotel during the 1986 renovation, with historic photos lining the walls. Open nightly, the bar serves specialty house martinis, vintage ports and cognac, fine wine, beer and cocktails. It also continues the famous tradition of weekend live jazz. You may spot the Gallery Bar in *The Italian Job, Rumor Has It*, and *Blow* with Johnny Depp and Penelope Cruz.

The Cognac Room is the intimate lounge for Gallery Bar guests—the glass cabinets showcase vintage cognacs and liqueurs from the hotel's early days, including samples of Biltmore Bourbon, a specialty-made house blend from the 1940s. (Of course, the hotel opened right in the middle of Prohibition, but once the Depression arrived the hotel bars were stocked with the best bonded liquor.) The two wood-carved, gilded and painted murals you see were originally a set of four that hung in the Gold Room, created by artist Anthony B. Heinsbergen around 1938. The images are based on the *Tales of the Arabian Nights*. Two were mysteriously lost, but these that remain have been meticulously restored by Heinsbergen's son.

The Galeria represents the main artery of the hotel: a 350-foot-long promenade that connects all the ballrooms with the main public spaces and guest elevators. I defy you to find a grander promenade anywhere in the world. Symbols of California abound in the decoration—images of bison from Indian-head nickels, teepees and sunbursts. The ceiling is made of hand-painted circular friezes and Renaissance-style coffers, gilded in gold and depicting Roman goddesses, Roman ruins and nymphs. All the ceiling murals in the hotel were hand-painted by Giovanni Smeraldi (after whom the restaurant is named), an Italian artist, made famous by his work at the Vatican, the White House and Grand Central Station in New York. He spent hours lying on his back on scaffolding to complete the work.

The Galeria was originally decorated with 17th century French tapestries, small tables with bronze statues, benches and chairs.

"Guests dressed to the nines—the Galeria was a place to see and be seen, as guests strolled the length of the corridor," said Eberhard. "The space was so popular with guests and locals that the hotel maître d' would hand out polite cards asking non-guests to move on lest the corridor become too overly crowded or vagrants make themselves too comfortable."

Next to the gift shop, you'll notice a glass historical case with some of the hotel's original china, an entire set of which is still brought out on very special occasions.

The Emerald Room is the original main dining room for hotel guests —the Emerald Room could seat up to 500 people! In keeping with the room's function, the decor features themes of hunt and harvest, with hand-painted rabbits, roosters, fish and fowl on the cast-plaster ceiling beams (restored in the 1980s). The beams also feature mermaids, dogs, and even a monkey. Gold medallions along two walls and Italian chandeliers with polished stones complete the Renaissance elegance of the room.

Today the Emerald Room offers a dramatic setting for receptions, meetings and weddings, and can accommodate up to 350 people comfortably for a reception.

Just adjacent and connecting to the Emerald is the Gold Room. Originally two rooms, it functioned as the exclusive dining room for the hotel's elite guests and visitors, who entered at the bottom level garden-like "Palm Room" and entered the intimate Supper Room on the upper level, which has now been opened up to combine the two sections. The ceiling is gold cast-plaster, and nine mirrored windows surrounded with gold leaf line the room. Gold sconces and a gold frieze contribute to the room's theme.

A small door behind one of the mirrored panels leads to a stairwell and secret passageway used to enable more recognizable guests to be whisked away to a hidden, tended bar to continue imbibing during Prohibition,1920-1933. (All right, there might have been a little alcohol available at the hotel during its first decade.)

If you've ever seen the 1973 film *The Sting* you may remember this room as the bookie joint. It was also featured in recent movies, *The Wedding Crashers* and *Rumor Has It*. Today, the stately room functions perfectly for receptions, accommodating either meeting or dining space, and can seat 300-350 people for receptions or banquets.

Probably the most famous space in the entire hotel is the Crystal Ballroom. It is designed in a neoclassical style with signature balconies on three sides, two original 12-foot-diameter and imported Austrian crystal chandeliers, and Smeraldi's masterpiece-painted ceiling featuring Roman gods and goddesses, angels, cupids and other mythical figures. It took seven months to complete and is completely seamless. The ceiling was meticulously restored in the 1980s and accurately reflects the design on the carpet below.

This is where the Academy of Motion Picture Arts and Sciences first met in 1927 to discuss plans for their new organization and where Louis B. Mayer suggested presenting achievement awards to colleagues in their industry—thus, the Oscars were born! Legend has it that MGM art director Cedric Gibbons, who was in attendance, immediately grabbed a linen Biltmore napkin and sketched the design for the Oscar statue on it. Nine Oscar banquets were held at the hotel during the Academy's early years (1931, 1935, 1936-39, 1941-43). In 1977 Bob Hope hosted the Academy's 50th anniversary banquet in this ballroom.

Films that were shot here include *A Star Is Born, Rocky III, The Bodyguard,* and *True Lies.* Today the ballroom is one of the city's most popular spaces for weddings and receptions, and can seat up to 600 people.

What became of the hotel's famous "Biltmore Bowl" you ask? The Biltmore Bowl was originally called the Sala d'Oro Ballroom and was actually the world's largest nightclub in its earliest days—in 1934, a year after the repeal of Prohibition—just $5 used to get you admission and a bottle of French champagne! It was the best entertainment venue in town, hosting the top swing and big bands of the era, often hosted by famed bandleader Spike Jones, and frequented by movie stars and socialites. Clark Gable, Bette Davis, Walt Disney, Shirley Temple, Ginger Rogers, Frank Capra, Judy Garland and Spencer Tracy all won Oscars in this very room.

The room looked quite different than it does today—the circumference was made of arched colonnades with rich drapery and a lavishly ornamented, patterned ceiling. In the 1950s, the Biltmore Bowl was divided horizontally to create the Regency Room below (now the exhibit hall). The upper room, which remains the Biltmore Bowl, was renovated several years ago for $3 million to restore some of the interior grandeur to the stage and with the addition of the enormous crystal chandelier. It is the hotel's largest meeting and banquet space, and still holds some great social events including the Grammy awards after party and the semi-final rounds of *American Idol.* You can see the original design of the room and the Oscar photos in the Historic Corridor upstairs.

The Tiffany Ballroom historically was named the Colonnade Room due to its colonnades that line the east and west sides of the stunning space. Originally an open corridor, it was a foyer to the grand Crystal Ballroom and later became a small ballroom itself. Exploration is the theme here, with relief sculptures and panels depicting Queen Isabella, Christopher Columbus and other Spanish explorers honoring California's heritage. The ceiling is hand-painted cast-plaster. Today it is the smallest of the ballrooms, but still beautiful in its own right. It can seat up to 300 people.

The entire South Galeria wing of the hotel wasn't completed until 1928. The inspiration for the decor came from the historic city of Pompeii, Italy with a vaulted ceiling, marble balustrades and heavy Roman piers. Gold-painted wrought iron gates open to a staircase leading down to the Biltmore Bowl. The floral friezes reflect the themes of the halls of Pompeii and were all hand-painted by Anthony Heinsbergen and restored in the 1980s.

The Regency Room used to be part of the high-ceiling Biltmore Bowl, but became the Regency Room in the 1950s. Today, it functions as an ideal space for exhibits and large meetings, and can accommodate up to 1,000 people. You will see original sections of the room near the stairwells and in the bathrooms.

The health club opened in 1926 as a men's club, designed to look like the deck of a luxury cruise ship, such as the Queen Mary, with solid brass trim on windows, doors and railings, teakwood deck chairs and hand-laid Italian mosaic tile on the walls and in the pool. The area outside the enclosed pool section once consisted of small, separated treatment rooms where guests could get massages, steam baths and other spa-type services considered ultimate luxury and state-of-the-art back in the 20s! All designs are of a nautical theme.

Today, the club is accessible exclusively to guests; that is, use is complimentary. Accessed via guestroom keycard, it is always stocked with fresh towels, and men's and women's locker rooms and showers are available for the guests' convenience. The health club has a dry sauna, steam room, Jacuzzi and fitness equipment including cardio machines, Stair Masters and treadmills as well as a full weight room.

The health club has been seen on the silver screen in *Bugsy* (starring

Warren Beatty), Ron Howard's *Cocoon* and *Cruel Intentions* with Reese Witherspoon.

The Millennium Biltmore's enormous kitchen space covers 25,000 square feet, and is equipped to serve 3,500 meals a day. There are actually five separate kitchens—one each for Room Service, Smeraldi's Restaurant, the former Grand Ave. Bar, Bugis Street Brasserie and a pastry kitchen. The main area is utilized for cooking for large events, and for banquet preparation.

The kitchens have created and served meals to U. S. presidents, international royalty from Europe to Japan, and of course, for the Oscars. They have served as the backdrop for television series like the steamy scene in a recent *Scandal*. The Millennium Biltmore archives have menus dating from the opening night of the hotel to the current time and have some fascinating facts. For example, in 1936, a full five-course steak dinner was just $1.50!

In the Historic Corridor just a small sample of some of the historical photos the hotel keeps in its archives are represented. In a large photo on the wall, you can see what the Biltmore Bowl looked like in its heyday. At the 1937 Academy Awards, the adjacent legend points out some of the more famous faces who attended that banquet, like Cecil B. DeMille and his wife, as well as Walt Disney, Tyrone Power, Henry Fonda and Spike Jones. Throughout the past few years numerous guests have helped identify some of the missing identities of people in the photo.

Along the Galeria, glass enclosures showcase some of the hotel memorabilia, including original china and silverware, menus, and other hotel collateral. The largest case once held the Biltmore Dress, a hand-painted silk gown modeled in both design and decoration after the Crystal Ballroom. It was often worn by Peggy Hamilton, a 1920s fashion designer and socialite nicknamed the "Biltmore Girl" for her constant presence at the hotel, where she would hold headlining fashion shows regularly.

Used primarily for meeting space and exhibits or as a reception area for events going on downstairs in the Bowl, the Heinsbergen Room is named, of course, after Anthony Heinsbergen, the artist who did much artwork around the hotel.

With space on both the tenth and eleventh floors of the hotel, the Presidential Suite is a two-story, 4,600 square-foot retreat that features three bedrooms, five marble bathrooms, a full kitchen, huge closets, a teakwood-paneled elevator, spiral staircase, library, grand piano, elegant formal dining room and spacious living quarters with plasma television. Pershing Square views and decorative fireplaces complete the expansive suite. Some of the Presidential Suite guests have included U. S. Presidents Franklin Roosevelt, Harry Truman, Lyndon Johnson, Gerald Ford, Jimmy Carter, Ronald Reagan and George Bush, Sr., as well as Ingrid Bergman, the Duke and Duchess of York, and most recently actors Jamie Foxx, Warren Beatty and Annette Bening.

There are two small buttons which trigger panels to open on the walls of the elevator—used during Prohibition as secret liquor compartments! (All right, there was a fair amount of imbibing going on at the hotel during its first decade, but only of the finest spirits!)

Smeraldi's occupies the spot that once served as the Men's Lounge on its western side and the Biltmore Soda Fountain on the eastern side, and was, of course, named after the artist Giovanni Smeraldi, who painted the spectacular murals around the hotel. The Men's Lounge opened off of the lobby (now the Rendezvous Court), and was inspired by the room in which Queen Isabella of Spain learned of Columbus's discoveries—hence images of notable Spaniards once graced the cast-plaster ceiling, which was lit by an illuminated globe modeled after one of Leonardo da Vinci's designs.

The following are some potpourri-ish press clippings and other pearls of information about the hotel that are gathered here to convey in a kaleidoscopic manner the almost radiant splendor of the Millennium Biltmore's palazzo-like interiors, then and now:

> *Like Peacock Alley in the old Waldorf Astoria, razed to make way for the Empire State Building, the 300-foot-long Galeria, which once was*

lined with sofas, was also lined with people watchers waiting to catch a glimpse of "the King" as Clark Gable was sometimes called as was long before that Rudolph Valentino.

The Millennium Biltmore is not without its well-hidden share of secret places. One is a waist-high door that's in one of the mirrored panels in the Gold Ballroom which during Prohibition provided easy exit for revelers drinking bootleg booze from teacups. There are secret panels in the Presidential Suite where bootleg liquor was available at the push of a button.

Lined with blue and cream-colored Italian tile and accented with brass, the Millennium Biltmore pool, now part of a full-service health club, was designed to recall an earlier era of splendor.

Originally a corridor to Grand Avenue, the opulent Gallery Bar has live jazz Friday and Saturday nights. Adjoining the Gallery Bar is the Cognac Room with its huge murals themed after Tales of the Arabian Nights, painted by Anthony B. Heinsbergen in the 1930s. Giovanni Smeraldi hand-painted murals in the ceiling of the Galeria and in 1947 restored some of them.

The *Host of the Coast* so beautifully describes the Galeria that I quote from it here:

"Described at the opening as "the very artery of the distinguished life of the Los Angeles Biltmore," the Galeria Real (in English, "royal gallery") is the hotel's main street. The 350-foot-long promenade, extending the building's full width, connects the meeting and banquet rooms with the hotel's public areas. In 1923 the Galeria's walls were covered with seventeenth-century French tapestries, deep-pile rugs softened steps on its marble floor, small tables held bronzes, and Spanish and Italian Renaissance furniture provided comfortable seating for visitors.

The glory of this grand arcade, reminiscent of a Venetian palace, is the ceiling, painted by Giovanni Smeraldi himself—lying on his back on lofty scaffolding. Here the artist chose to link California's history with its Castilian [Spain] heritage and ancient classical traditions. Divided into nine sections, the ceiling alternates Renaissance-style coffers with circular friezes illustrating winged horses, dancing nymphs, Roman ruins, and some white-robed goddesses in cameo roles. Bronze filigree work is interspersed with the spokelike paintings. High above elaborate recessed entrances to the banquet room are reliefs of two satyrs with coats of arms displaying American motifs: a bison, an Indian tepee, a sunburst, and the Indian head from the American nickel. Angels fly throughout the Galeria on column capitals and the circular ceiling friezes. Satyrs and fruits of the earth's bounty are sculpted onto the columns."

"It is the Galeria Real which will cause the Los Angeles Biltmore to be discussed and remembered wherever smart people gather." (Los Angeles Biltmore Souvenir, 1923)

"The Galeria serves as the Millennium Biltmore's chief thoroughfare—one of the most famous hotel promenades in the world. Decorative gates, guarded by more angels, lead to the Gold Room. Grape leaves and satyrs on columns signify unmatched hospitality." (Host of the Coast)

"Built to an ideal, this great mass of steel, mortar, brick and countless other materials blossomed into a magnificent flower of architectural perfection. The wonders of its public salons are worthy of the finest cathedrals or of kings' palaces." (Los Angeles Biltmore Souvenir, 1923)

"Utterly sumptuous glory, monarchical chairs in $50 a yard brocades with throne-like mien, ceilings tricked out by veritable artists in subtle allegory...massive bronzes, priceless tapestries, art deluxe, luxury

heaped upon luxury—for of such is the new Biltmore composed. ..."
(Alma Whitmaker, Los Angeles Times, October 1, 1923)

The hotel's E-shaped wings allowed most of the guests to have an exceptional bird's-eye view of Pershing Square (or so says an old postcard). They entered right off the park on Olive Street, the original main entrance. Beneath the red brick façade ornamented with cream-colored stone, tall arches framed by Corinthian pilasters directed attention to the elaborate doorway. There, surrounded by heroic Ionic columns holding a magnificent frieze, a uniformed doorman was always on duty. Retail stores gave passersby plenty of opportunities for window shopping.

Again, I quote from *Host of the Coast* which so eloquently describes other areas of the hotel including the Emerald and Gold Rooms:

Four hundred persons could dine here in splendor in the Millennium Biltmore's early days or dance away the evening when the tables were moved out. Originally the hotel's main dining room, the Emerald Room (previously named the Renaissance Room) is framed by two striking arcades of faux travertine columns. On the handpainted beams of the cast-plaster ceiling are harvest and hunt motifs: from rabbits to roosters, fish to fowl. Tall arched windows reflect the light of the four Italian chandeliers with polished stones. Along the north and south walls run a row of gold medallions, and decorative grilles are illuminated by half-moon sconces.

In the Millennium Biltmore's early years, this majestic 5,500-square-foot room accommodated hundreds of diners. Under an egg-and-dart molding, mermaids cavort on a frieze supported by massive columns topped with Ionic capitals. A series of hunting images runs along the underside. The ceiling, with its handpainted plaster beams, was also decorated with animals—even an exotic monkey made its way into the pastoral scene.

The Biltmore served as a rest and recreation facility for US service-

men during World War II with the entire second floor used for overnight stays. Los Angeles grew faster than any metropolitan area in the country during this same boom time. And women joined the workforce in L.A. and other cities in unprecedented numbers. In L.A. alone, "women grew to comprise as much as 60 percent of the workforce," historian Doris Kearns Goodwin notes in her book No Ordinary Time, about President Franklin Roosevelt's home front during the war.

Two original crystal-laced chandeliers, twelve feet in diameter, hang from the shallow dome of the ceiling and give the Crystal Ballroom its name.

On three sides of the room, intimate balconies rest between tall columns topped by golden capitals. The ceiling, painted in the Roman style of the first century, is one of Giovanni Smeraldi's masterpieces. During restorations in the 1970s and 1980s, it was cleaned and fresh gold leaf was applied to reinvigorate his contribution.

Bas-relief sculptures of Queen Isabella and Christopher Columbus welcome guests to the spectacular room defined by gilded columns and graceful half-moon balconies. Neoclassical in style, the 6,300-square-foot ballroom, also the work of Anthony B. Heinsbergen, can seat 700. The 29-foot-high domed ceiling is covered with a galaxy of mythical figures and heavenly bodies painted by Giovanni Smeraldi. He and his crew reportedly worked seven months to complete the seamless mural on canvas, which includes Ceres, the goddess of agriculture. Early Roman in style, the decoration resembles Raphael's work at the Vatican, where Smeraldi himself apprenticed. Beneath the ceiling is an elaborate border of ornamental plaster.

When the Millennium Biltmore was young, weekly fashion shows and the annual masquerade Bachelors' Ball took over the ballroom. In years since, the hotel's premier room has been seen often in movies and on television. It served as the fight arena for Sylvester Stallone in Rocky III in 1981. In 1989 the breathtaking space served as the stage for the actress Michelle Pfeiffer, where she stood atop the grand *piano in* The Fabulous Baker Boys, *a performance that earned her an Oscar nomination. Founded in this room in 1927, the Academy of Motion Picture Arts and Sciences held its fiftieth anniversary here in 1977. Many of the Hollywood stars and moguls who had been at the inaugural banquet were present again, from Mary Pickford to Jack L. Warner and Darryl F. Zanuck. Bob Hope served as the master of ceremonies, a role he had performed fifteen times before.*

When the hotel opened in 1923, guests were welcomed in what is now the Rendezvous Court. Fountains and lush foliage have long created a gardenlike atmosphere for visitors entering from Pershing Square. The vaulted Spanish Renaissance ceiling and the grand staircase leading to the Churrigueresque-style doorway are the work of Anthony B. Heinsbergen, who assisted Giovanni Smeraldi in designing the elegant interiors.

Schultze and Weaver wanted the original lobby to be one of the hotel's most pleasing rooms, presenting "an air of business and a distinct feeling of masculine possession." When guests step from the park into what is now the Rendezvous Court, this four-story space even today makes the 'perfect introduction to the smart life' that the architects envisioned.' Pausing here for afternoon tea or cocktails with piano music, one might be in a Spanish cathedral.

Giovanni Smeraldi's assistant Anthony B. Heinsbergen produced an elaborate Moorish ceiling of plaster with wood beams. Rams and cherubs on high join a frieze of Spanish coats of arms and figures of griffins with heraldic shields. The two bronze and crystal chandeliers were imported from Italy in 1923. Tapestries originally draped the travertine stone walls, which were warmed by bronze floodlights, and custom-woven rugs covered the marble floor.

Monumental arcades on either side lead the eye toward the far end of the space. There, a double staircase capped with a cast-iron grille rises to the old "society floor" of the hotel. Los Angeles's namesake angels star here and hint at their role throughout the hotel in bas reliefs, column capitals, and decorative paintings. At the top of the stairs is Heinsbergen's grand doorway—almost an altar—re-

splendent with elaborate surface decoration in the Churrigueresque, or Spanish baroque, style. Ceres and Balboa, both featured outside the Olive Street entrance, reappear here. Astrological motifs distinguish the clock in the arch, which has told the time since 1923. To the architectural historian Robert Winter, the room's lavish features are "sensational monuments of an opulent age."

The last word about the first days of this great hotel also goes to the effervescent *Host of the Coast* by Margaret Leslie Davis:

A week-long celebration marked the opening of the Millennium Biltmore. Among those attending were the heads of some of the largest hotels in the country. With John McEntee Bowman and James Woods, vice president of the Biltmore Company, they left Grand Central Terminal in New York City on September 19, 1923, arriving in Los Angeles twelve days later. The hotel's general manager, Charles Baad, greeted them with a flourish. Private parties at the Millennium Biltmore were hosted by the architects Leonard Schultze and Fullerton Weaver and by the owners of the Scofield Engineering-Construction Company. On Saturday, September 29, 50,000 specially invited members of the public were given a preview of the hotel.

The hotel's formal dedication, a dinner for 500 male guests, was held on October 1 and featured no fewer than 25 speakers, broadcast live on radio. Woods pledged that the hotel would meet the "standards of decency, efficiency, and fair treatment to all." The evening concluded with an impassioned speech by the famed lawyer William Jennings Bryan, who declared that the new Millennium Biltmore, by giving ideas and creating ideals for the furnishings of Los Angeles homes, would make the city a "better and more wonderful place in which to live."

2

Adding to Prosperity: The Millennium Biltmore Addition

When the Millennium Biltmore readied to expand on its success in the late '20s with a brand new, mammoth extension, the West Coast press lit up with excitement, praise and not a little local chest-thumping.

BILTMORE LETS CONTRACT FOR $3 MILLION JOB
(August 5, 1927)

Work On 12-Story Addition Will Start About August 25; Planned 517 Rooms, Huge Dance Floor.

Involving approximately $3 million, the Scofield Engineering-Construction Company has been awarded the contract for the erection of the new heights-limit addition to the Biltmore Hotel.

According to E. T. Heltschmidt, representative of the architects, Schultze & Weaver, ground for the new unit will be broken about August 25.

12 STORIES PLANNED

Plans show that the structure will be twelve stories and basement in height to house 517 guestrooms. One of the features of the building will be a ballroom, 140 by 107 feet.

The new addition will front on Grand Avenue, extending

from the Biltmore Theatre on the north to the end of the existing building on the south.

A building on part of the site, used as executive offices for the hotel, will be torn down.

HOTEL ADDITION STEEL GOING UP
(L. A. Examiner, no date recorded)

Much progress is being made on the erection of steel for the framework of the $3,600,000 addition to the Biltmore Hotel and the work is to be completed February 1, according to the Scofield Engineering-Construction Company which is erecting the structure.

It was explained by the contractors that Gladding, McBean & Co. will make first deliveries on terra-cotta, face brick, roof and hollow tile, on the 15th inst. Although the material will not be used immediately on delivery, it was pointed out that it was desired to have the material on hand ahead of schedule, to speed up work in hope of having the structure completed before September 30, the next, the date set.

(*The Daily National Hotel Reporter,* date not recorded)

Active work will soon begin upon the big new addition to the big Biltmore Hotel in Los Angeles. The new structure will be of the same exterior architecture as the present hotel, and will contain, in addition to 500 splendid rooms with bath, two more "galleries" similar in design to those in the present hotel, a mammoth ballroom, one of the finest in the country, eleven more private dining rooms, a new office suite for general manager Woods and his executive staff, also a new print shop and other working departments. As the *Daily National Hotel Reporter* has already remarked, there never has been opened in this country a hotel which has received more universal praise from professionals and laymen than the Los Angeles Biltmore. We cannot recall a single adverse comment among the hundreds which have come to us, spoken and by letter, from patrons of the establishment, dating back from its opening and up to the present time. John McE. Bowman, head of the great Bowman-Biltmore system, expressed great satisfaction with the showing made by the Los Angeles hotel when he returned from the Pacific Coast a few weeks ago, particularly expressing himself as gratified at the record made by his long-time associate, Mister Jas. Woods, vice president and general manager of the Bowman-Biltmore hotels in Los Angeles and Santa Barbara.

TILE BEING SET ON ROOF OF NEW HOTEL ADDITION

(*L. A. Examiner*, no date recorded)

With the awarding of contracts yesterday, the work is to start immediately on setting ornamental and roof tile for the new $3,600,000 addition to the Biltmore Hotel, now being erected on Grand Avenue at the rear of the present structure.

In order to make the roof of the structure available as a promenade if it is desired, it is being paved and decorated with ornamental tile, according to the contractors, Scofield Engineering-Construction Company. Workmen have just started the job of setting 450 tons of terra-cotta and 600,000 faced brick on the exteriors, supplied from the kilns of Gladding, McBean & Co. The same concern also is supplying all the hollow tile, decorative and roof tile.

James Woods, vice-president of the Los Angeles Biltmore, announced that 500 rooms would be added to the Millennium Biltmore. "It would be built," it was announced in a contemporary news account, "at the rear of the present hotel now used as a parking station, and on the site of the four-story administration building of the Millennium Biltmore, which will be razed to clear the lot."

WILL HAVE TWO PARK FRONTS

"This will give a complete block frontage from the Pacific Mutual building to the Biltmore Theatre, and the addition will present a new façade for the hotel, facing on the recently com-

Construction almost complete

pleted public library and the lawns of Library Park. The hotel will then have two park frontages, Pershing Square on one side and Library Park on the other, accenting the location as the finest hotel site in Los Angeles.

"The plans provide for connecting the north and south corridors to extend through the building; the installations of three more passenger elevators, making nine in all; and to continue the general character, style and harmony of the present Millennium Biltmore throughout the addition.

Adding to Prosperity: The Biltmore Addition

"The top floor, facing on Grand Avenue, is planned for permanent apartments of generous size, several of which have already been applied for. Beautiful suites, with rooms considerably larger than those in the present house are planned for the street frontage on all floors, some of the rooms being 16x18 feet in size.

"The main public floor will be on the corresponding level with the present Galeria Real, and will be connected with it by two galleries extending from Grand Avenue. These galleries will be twenty-one feet in width and will be paneled with wood and stone, and furnished and decorated to conform with the present Galeria.

"They will be flanked with smart shops, and the south one will have two grand staircases 18 feet in width leading from it to the grand ballroom.

"The grand ballroom, the largest in any hotel in America, 140x107 feet in size, will be surrounded on three sides by balcony boxes, will be beautifully decorated, and will seat 1800 diners at banquet in the main hall, and can care for two hundred more in the connecting foyer.

"This ballroom will be reached by an automobile ramp when it is desired to use it for motor car shows or other exhibitions. A movable platform can be raised from, or lowered into, the floor at one end, for the accommodation of speakers and entertainment purposes. On the north side of the ball room a special banquet kitchen is planned for the sole care of the business of this room. Beneath the ballroom will be a basement which will furnish locker and toilet rooms for guests, and a large room especially for the waiters who are employed for banquets. There will also be table and chair storage rooms on this floor."

The mid 1920s brought a boom in hotel business throughout the

United States. Los Angeles was certainly no exception. The Millennium Biltmore catered to approximately 200 new guests per day, according to the *Los Angeles Times.*

"With the dawn of the New Year, Los Angeles stands poised on the threshold of a tourist season which in the estimate of managers of leading hotels promises to excel every year since 1915, with the exception of the record-breaking season of 1922.

"With very few exceptions, and those only among smaller houses, almost every prominent tourist hotel in the city showed a substantial increase in registrations in 1925 compared with 1924. The advances range from 10 to 13 percent, the average increase being approximately 12 to 13 percent.

"Statistics on 1925 reservations issued by the managers of 15 hotels show that these houses catered to approximately 500,000 guests. Conservative estimates place the number of tourists handled by hotels in general well over the 2,000,000 mark.

"The Millennium Biltmore Hotel catered to about 200 new guests per day, aggregating 73,000 for the entire year, according to Manager Charles Baad's figures, which include reservations up to December 26.

The situation at the Ambassador Hotel is somewhat different than at other local hotels, according to Manager Abe Frank. The Ambassador, he pointed out, has 325 permanent guests. Nevertheless the Wilshire boulevard house catered to approximately 40,000 transients in 1925,

Crystal Ballroom

which Frank estimates to be a 20 per cent increase over the previous year.

"The Alexandria, a downtown hotel, with more than 100 rooms occupied by permanent residents, handled a transient tourist business of 55,000. Harold Lathrop, manager, estimated the 1925 increase at about 13 percent."

In the lovely book, *The Los Angeles Biltmore: Host of the Coast,*

Hotel with Pershing Square as it originally looked

published on the hotel's seventy-fifth anniversary, various restorations were highlighted.

In 1969, the Millennium Biltmore was designated a historic and cultural monument by the Los Angeles Cultural Heritage Board, but by then the city's business and social center was moving west. The grand

hotel no longer attracted the world leaders, movie stars, athletes, and aviators who had once been such eager guests.

The Millennium Biltmore was sold in 1976 to the architects Phyllis Lambert of Montreal and Gene Summers of Laguna Beach, who undertook a $30 million renovation. The lobby, Music Room, Renaissance (Emerald) Room, Gold Room, and Galeria were cleaned and restored, with special care taken to protect Smeraldi's works, and the guest rooms were upgraded.

The Millennium Biltmore's social sparkle was coming back to life as well. It hosted the Oscars' fiftieth anniversary party in 1977 and a farewell luncheon for president-elect Ronald Reagan in January 1981. During the 1984 summer Olympic Games, the International Olympic Committee set up headquarters in the hotel.

Under the later ownership of Biltmore Partners, the building in the mid-1980s became the centerpiece of Biltmore Place, a project that included further restoration of the landmark and construction of an adjacent office tower. Anthony T. Heinsbergen was put in charge of cleaning and refurbishing the artwork created in part by his father, Anthony B. Heinsbergen. The ceiling in the Crystal Ballroom was washed with a special formula to remove smoke and dirt, then retouched. According to the Los Angeles Conservancy, a coat of buttermilk was applied to the murals for a uniform sheen and further protection.

In 2000, a two-year, multimillion-dollar renovation updated all guest rooms, including the club levels; refurbished the Biltmore Bowl and other meeting and exhibition space; and converted the Imperial Suite into the five-room Executive Boardroom. In 2008 the landmark—which the city's Cultural Heritage Board has likened to "a sturdy art gallery, connecting early California history and folklore to the brilliant years of the Spanish Renaissance"—celebrated its eighty-fifth anniversary on October 2 with a gala dinner in the Crystal Ballroom.

In 1976, on a visit to Los Angeles, Vice-President Nelson A. Rockefeller was presented with a wall frieze created especially for the Millennium Biltmore Hotel by the nationally known artist, Jim Dine. Making the presentation was John McKennon, general manager of the Millennium Biltmore.

"Many facets of Dine's work, sculpture, watercolors, wall friezes, will be featured in the Millennium Biltmore's current renovation and restoration programs. They will highlight guest rooms, suites and guest room corridors," one hotel executive said at the time.

3

The Biltmore Theatre

The Biltmore Theatre opened on March 3, 1924 with a show called *Sally, Irene and Mary*. Comedian Will Rogers emceed the opening. Like the adjacent hotel itself, the Biltmore Theatre was designed by Leonard Schultze and S. Fullerton Weaver. With its main entrance on 5th Street, the theater was also connected to the hotel via an arcade. The marquee of the theater was "Erlanger's Biltmore" after Erlanger and his partner Mark Telaw teamed with ex-producer Charles Froman and others to form the theatrical syndicate, which controlled many theatrical interests and businesses. They also built several Broadway theaters in New York, including what is now the St. James Theatre on W. 44th St.

The *Los Angeles Times* put the importance of the Biltmore Theatre in perspective in this article:

NEW PLAYHOUSE TO SUPPLY NEED
Biltmore Theatre Follows Modern Lines. Intimacy and Capacity to Be Provided. Higher Quality of Shows Here Predicted.
By Edwin Schallert

The need for a modern Playhouse that will have both intimacy and capacity promises at last to be filled in the instance of the Biltmore Theatre, under construction. The building follows up

Biltmore Theatre. Will Rogers was keynote speaker for opening.

to date lines of similar edifices in New York in that it has lateral depth, and will permit the auditor to "feel" the drama through the closeness to the stage, as well as to hear and see most satisfactorily.

No other theater in the city brings out these advantages in

quite the same way. Most of them date in construction nearly a decade ago. In the meanwhile styles in theaters have changed, and the manner of presentation has naturally correspondingly altered.

It is probable that with the completion of the Biltmore many more shows of a higher quality will be attracted to the Coast. They will find conditions more suitable to their production, and consequently will afford a better entertainment to the audiences. There is reason to anticipate, therefore, that the public's interest in attending the spoken drama will be stimulated.

SHOWS TO COME INTACT. The policy of the Biltmore Theatre will be a development of that which has distinguished the Mason. It will be the official theater for road attractions. It will house the productions of Erlanger, Selwyn, Sam Harris, John Golden, the Shuberts and dozens of other prominent New York managers.

When the theater opens in January, one of the premier Manhattan offerings will be brought to the Coast intact, to set the proper precedent for the future. New York managers have lost faith, it is said, in sending what are known as second companies to the Coast, and the beginning of the Biltmore's career is expected to cause a change in the system in vogue.

POSITION RECOGNIZED. The importance of Los Angeles as a theatergoing center is now generally recognized in the East. It is further understood that the large professional audience in

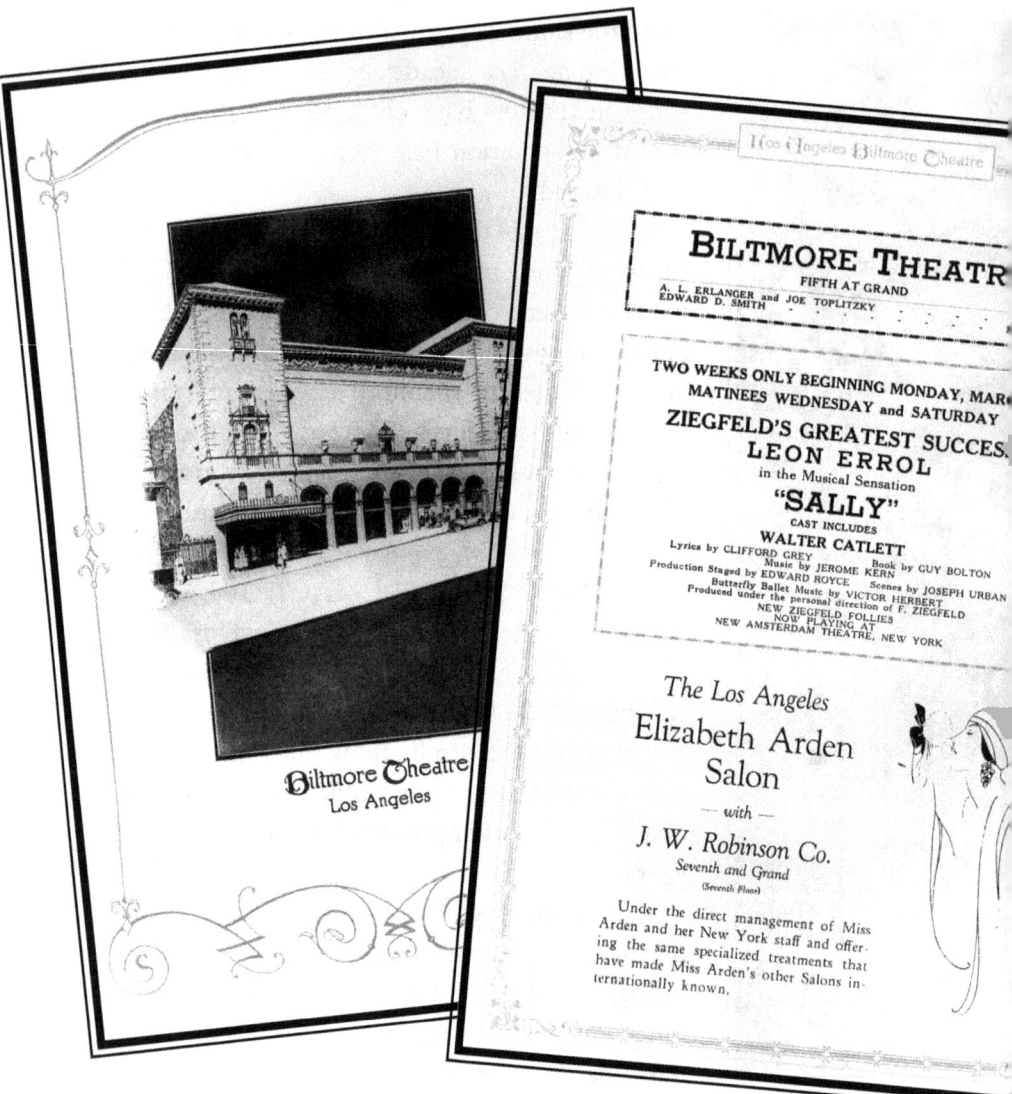

Biltmore Theatre posters. The theater was raised in 1967 and replaced by the Biltmore office tower in 1986.

this section of the West demands the best in entertainment, and the intention is to entrench the road production through suitable surroundings, as well as the improvement in plays and casts.

A new theater in a central location will have an important airing on the future trend of the theatrical district. The Biltmore opens up what is virtually a new sector. The nearest theaters at present are the Philharmonic Auditorium, which is dedicated to music, and Grauman's Metropolitan and the Criterion, which are given over to high class picture entertainment. Pershing Square promises eventually to become the center of artistic activity, as represented by this theater.

The theaters in this vicinity are all easy of access, and their accessibility will be improved through the proposed subway construction.

VALUE IN CONCENTRATION. There is value in this sort of concentration. It increases patronage, and the interest in the art of entertainment. The worth of the enterprises centered here will add to the artistic development of the entire community.

Attractions that probably will be booked at the Biltmore about the time of its opening include "Lightin'," the famous show in which the late Frank Bacon starred; "The Merchant of Venice" with David Warfield; and lighter offerings like "The Gingham Girl" and "The Clinging Vine."

It is probable that "The Merchant of Venice" will open the new theater or if this is not available at that time some other especially elaborate offering will be transported directly to Los Angeles from New York.

The opening of the Biltmore Theatre is probably going to mean a doubling of roadshow presentations here, and the plans are to continue the policy at the Mason now prevailing. Many productions which have heretofore been booked for only one week will play two, and others that have had success during two weeks may continue for three and four.

If this system can once be soundly established, it will mean a constant improvement in the attractions that are brought out from the East. The New York managers will be right in the mood for sending out their best casts and plays if they can be assured of runs in the larger cities on the Coast that will enable them to derive an enlarged return.

The Visit, a play by Frederick Durrenmatt, was first produced on Broadway in 1955. It is a drama about a wealthy older lady who seeks revenge on an erstwhile love by offering one million francs to townspeople to kill him. It also had a successful post-Broadway tour. It won the New York Drama Critics Circle Award as Best Foreign Play before its extended tour started in Wilmington, Delaware, in 1959. The tour of "that turned out to be a surprise, commercial success," wrote Jerrod Brown in his book *The Fabulous Land*. "Indeed, in Los Angeles. The balcony of the Biltmore Theatre was reopened after many years in order to accommodate the requests for tickets."

4

It Happened Many Nights: The Oscars at the Millennium Biltmore

The first Oscars may have been at the Roosevelt but the organizational banquet was held at the Millennium Biltmore on May 11, 1927. Perhaps the biggest Oscar night at the Millennium Biltmore or any other place was when *It Happened One Night* won for Best Picture in the seventh year of the Academy Awards. Clark Gable won for Best Actor and Claudette Colbert as Best Actress. The award to Gable would make him the biggest star in Hollywood and lead to his role as Rhett Butler in *Gone with the Wind*. The Oscar also, despite the movie's commercial success, made Gable a genuine artist in everyone's eyes.

Let's go back nearly 80 years to February 27, 1935 and the Academy Awards. Irvin S. Cobb was the Master of Ceremonies. Shirley Temple received the first Juvenile Award at age 6, from Walt Disney, becoming the youngest Oscar recipient ever. Frank Capra's romantic comedy *It Happened One Night* became the first film to perform a "clean sweep" of the top five award categories: Best Picture, Best Director, Best Actor, Best Actress, and Best Screenplay. Clark Gable won Best Actor, and the Oscar would help Gable become a top star for decades. Claudette Colbert won Best Actress and the film itself Best Picture. The Best Picture winner was also the Academy's first romantic comedy winner. I remember when my father, the late columnist and drama critic, Ward Morehouse, interviewed Gable at length, when *The Misfits* with Mari-

Idea for "Oscar" first scribbled on hotel napkin

lyn Monroe was being shot in Nevada many years later. All Gable could talk about was was being on Broadway in the 1920s.

Irving S. Cobb was a star in his own right—a journalist star. He worked at *The Evening Sun* in 1904, where he covered the Russian-Japanese peace conference. His performance garnered a job offer from Joseph Pulitzer's *New York World* where he became the highest-paid reporter in the United States. He also was a published short story writer, with one of his stories made into *The Woman Accused* with Cary Grant.

Unlike all the media exposure and hoopla with today's Academy Awards, the first Oscar ceremony was a banquet at the Hollywood Roosevelt Hotel, with Academy President Douglas Fairbanks passing out the golden statuettes...tickets for guests were for $5. The fourth Academy Awards, in 1931, moved to the Sala d'Oro in the Millennium Biltmore honoring movies made from August 1, 1930 to July 31, 1931. Lionel Barrymore won the Best Actor award for his performance playing a defense attorney defending his daughter's ex-boyfriend on charges of murdering the gangster who was her ex-lover. While Barrymore won the Oscar for the film mainly because of a long courtroom monologue, it helped catapult Clark Gable's rise to stardom in subsequent films. It also marked the first appearance of Gable and Leslie Howard, a major star at the time, who would play Ashley Wilkes to Gable's Rhett Butler.

The second-to-last Academy Awards held at the Millennium Biltmore Bowl was on February 26, 1942. Bob Hope was the Master of Ceremonies. The ceremony is considered notable as the year in which *Citizen Kane* didn't win Best Picture. Best Picture of the Year was awarded to *How Green Was My Valley*, the story of Welsh coal miners. John Ford won his third Academy Award for Best Director, also for

Legend has it Shirley Temple, in presenting the Oscar to Walt Disney, at first wouldn't let go of it!

Clark Gable accepting the Best Actor Oscar in 1935 in the film "It Happened One Night" costarring Claudette Colbert who won the Best Actress Oscar.

Spencer Tracy and Bette Davis accept Academy Awards

How Green Was My Valley. Welles won along with Herman J. Mankiewicz for Best Original Screenplay. Controversy whirled around Welles, not only about the movie's loose depiction of newspaper czar William Randolph Hearst, but about whether Welles really deserved a screenwriting credit for the picture.

Most public attention was focused on the Best Actress race between sibling rivals Joan Fontaine in Alfred Hitchcock's *Suspicion* and Olivia DeHaviland to have one for *Hold Back the Dawn*. Fontaine's victory was the only time an actor won for a performance in an Alfred Hitchcock film.

This was also the first year in which documentaries were included. The first Oscar for a documentary was awarded to *Churchill's Island*.

The Little Foxes established a new high of nine nominations without winning a single Oscar. This mark was matched by *Peyton Place* in

1957, and exceeded by *The Turning Point* and *The Color Purple*, both of which received eleven nominations without a win.

The 8th Academy Awards were held on March 5, 1936, at the Millennium Biltmore Hotel in Los Angeles, California. They were hosted by Frank Capra. This was the first year in which the gold statuettes were called "Oscars."

The short-lived category of Best Dance Direction was introduced this year. The DGA successfully lobbied for its elimination three years later.

Mutiny on the Bounty became the last film to date to win Best Picture, and nothing else.

This was the second and last year that write-in votes were allowed at the Oscars. *A Midsummer Night's Dream* became the only film to have ever won a write-in Oscar. It won Best Cinematography.

The 9th Academy Awards were held on March 4, 1937, at the Millennium Biltmore Hotel in Los Angeles, California. They were hosted

more Oscar festivities

ABOVE: Betty Grable (blond) and former child star Jackie Coogan. BELOW: Former Olympics swimming star and "Tarzan" Johnny Weismuller

by George Jessel. The ceremony marked the first time in which the categories of Best Supporting Actor and Actress were awarded.

My Man Godfrey became the first film to receive nominations in all four acting categories. It also remains the only film not to get a Best Picture nomination despite four acting nods.

The 1937 Best Actress winner, Luise Rainier, is as of 2013 the earli-

LEFT: Judy Garland and Mickey Rooney at the 1939 Oscars.

BELOW: Best Actress Winner Joan Fontaine 1941 and Ginger Rogers.

LEFT: Born Margarita Carmen Cansino, Rita Hayworth became one of the biggest stars of the 1940s and 1950s. She starred in "Gilda," opposite Glenn Ford. In the film, she did a striptease which was quite provocative for the time but tame today.

est nominee or winner in any acting category who is still living. She also holds the record for longest-lived acting winner ever, at age 103.

Bob Hope at 50th anniversary party of Academy Awards

It Happened Many Nights: The Oscars at the Biltmore   71

The 10th Academy Awards were held on March 10, 1938, at the Millennium Biltmore Hotel. Originally scheduled to be held on March 3, 1938, the ceremony was postponed due to heavy flooding in Los Angeles. The host of the ceremony was Bob Burns.

This was the last year in which the categories of Best Dance Direction and Best Assistant Director were awarded. The former provides the only nomination ever received by a Marx Brothers film (David Gould for the dance number, "All God's Children Got Rhythm" in *A Day at the Races*).

The Life of Emile Zola became the first film to receive ten nominations.

With her Best Actress award for *The Good Earth*, Luise Rainier became the first actor ever to receive two Academy Awards. She also became the first actor to win consecutive awards.

A Star Is Born was the very first color film ever to receive a Best Picture nomination.

This is the first year the Irving G. Thalberg Memorial Award was given. The first recipient, Darryl F. Zanuck, holds the record for most Thalbergs with three.

The 13th Academy Awards honored American film achievements in 1940. This was the first year that sealed envelopes were used to keep secret the names of the winners which led to the famous phrase: "May I have the envelope, please." The accounting firm of Price Waterhouse was hired to count the ballots, after the fiasco of the leaked voting results in 1939 by the *Los Angeles Times*.

For the first time, the award for Best Screenplay was split into two separate categories: Best Original Screenplay and Best Adapted Screenplay.

Independent producer David O. Selznick, who had produced the previous year's big winner, *Gone with the Wind* (1939), also produced the Best Picture winner in 1940, *Rebecca* and campaigned heavily for its win. Selznick was the first to produce two consecutive winners of the Best Picture Oscar. Although *Rebecca* had eleven nominations, it only won for Best Picture and Best Cinematography (Black and White).

United Artists was the last of the original film studios (the others were MGM, Columbia, 20th Century Fox, Warner Bros., Universal, and Paramount) to win the Best Picture Oscar. *Rebecca* was the first American-made film directed by Alfred Hitchcock, and the only film from him to win Best Picture. Hitchcock actually had two films in the running, for in addition to *Rebecca* his *Foreign Correspondent* was also in the running for Best Picture.

1941 Oscar Firsts.

For the first time, names of all winners remained secret until the moment they received their awards.

Franklin D. Roosevelt gave a six minute direct radio address to the attendees from the White House. It is the first time an American president participated in the event.

Even after the Oscars event itself stopped serving hot entrees and had moved on to the larger environs of the Dorothy Chandler Pavilion, Oscar did not forget his first romance with the Millennium Biltmore. When the 1970s rolled around and the golden anniversary of the event was being planned, the Millennium Biltmore was once again the venue of first choice. Or, as it was reported breathlessly in the local press at the time:

"Oscars Birthday Party, the 50th anniversary of the founding of the Academy of Motion Picture Arts and Sciences, was held recently at the newly renovated Biltmore Hotel in Los Angeles. The luncheon fête, which featured a 4' x 5' birthday cake made by the hotel's pastry chef, was attended by more than 300 giants of the motion picture industry and was held in the hotel's Crystal Ballroom, site of the Academy's founding dinner in 1927. Pausing to chat over old times were Gene Summers, President of the Biltmore, and comedian Bob Hope."

My favorite scene in *The Fabulous Baker Boys*, starring Michelle Pfeiffer and Jeff and Beau Bridges, is with Pfeiffer singing *Makin' Whoopee*. The characters played by Pfeiffer and Jeff Bridges first make love at the Millennium Biltmore. The film, which is a favorite of people to watch on New Year's Eve, when it partially takes place, made a big star of Pfeiffer. Running into Jeff Bridges in New York not long ago I told him *The Fabulous Baker Boys* was one of my favorite movies. "Mine, too!" he replied, flashing that famous Bridges smile. Today, the Millennium Biltmore features some great jazz every Friday and Saturday nights but at least when I was there I didn't see anyone singing who remotely looked like Michelle Pfeiffer.

The 1938 Oscar ceremony at the Millennium Biltmore was momentarily jolted by security men who "smashed through the door of a (radio) booth with axes" to halt an illegal broadcast announcing the winners, according to author David Sheward in his book *The Big Book of Show Business Awards*. Humphrey Bogart attended some Oscar ceremonies at the Millennium Biltmore but when he won his Oscar for Best Actor in *Casablana* the ceremony had moved to the Coconut Grove in the Ambassador Hotel. Bogart had quite a sense of humor despite his tough guy image in many movies, especially his earlier ones. He also was a producer on the film *Knock On Any Door* costarring a young John Derek. Jeffrey Lyons, in his book *Stories My Father Told Me*, based on his late father's *New York Post* column "The Lyons Den," says Bogart was at New York's Stork Club restaurant when Harry Cohn, the head of Columbia Pictures, whispered something to him about the movie at the restaurant. And Lyons says Bogart told his wife, Lauren Bacall, that *Knock On Any Door* was a hit. "How do you know?" Bacall asked. Bogart, according to Lyons, said "he referred to the picture as 'Our movie.' If he had said, 'Your movie,' it means the picture was a flop."

5

Thelma Becker, Queen of the Millennium Biltmore, and Other Stars at the Hotel

Meet the Queen of the Millennium Biltmore, Thelma Becker. Thelma Becker lived at the hotel for nearly a half century. "I first picked the Biltmore because it was the leading hotel in town when I came," Becker told Bob Pool, a *Los Angeles Times* staff writer in 1988. "This was the center of town. Everything revolved around this place. I liked it and never wanted to leave. Even after I retired."

"There were things like the National Mosquito Convention. Seriously, they seemed to have a convention for every animal there is," she continued to *The Times*.

"I think the hotel is nicer now than it was then," she continued. "I think we have more things going on downtown now than we did back then. I'm very pleased with all the modern buildings we have now."

"Everything I need is here. I guess I'm just a city girl." Far away from her royal court. It was as if she was memorializing their oh so hot former love.

According to the *Los Angeles Times*:

"Thelma Becker checked into the Biltmore on Jan. 7, 1940, and never checked out.

"She was a lingerie saleswoman from Indiana, fresh out of college and looking for a place to stay while she set up a West Coast merchandising system for her company.

"The Los Angeles hotel was a place with clean rooms for $7 a night, convenient shops off its lobby and a handy location in the middle of downtown.

"In the 48 years since then, the Biltmore has become a legendary city landmark.

"In its ornate, marble-trimmed lobbies and hallways, Becker has herself become something of legend. The 73-year-old is the Biltmore's lone permanent resident. She has the run of the luxury hotel, which has 700 guest rooms, 22 banquet rooms, restaurants and bars—and room rates ranging from $120 to $1,500 a night.

"Becker has her own rate—the one-of-a-kind, $33-per-night "Thelma Becker Rate"—for a room with bath, according to hotel employees, many of whom treat her like a special family member.

"Over the years, Becker's ninth-floor window has given her a grandstand view of the city's evolution from low-rise to high-tech, high-rise.

"Her neighbors over the years have included presidents, Hollywood stars, royalty and thousands of convention-goers, many of whom romped the hostelry's hallways wearing silly hats.

"Every employee rates a cheery hello when they meet Becker in hallways and elevators. As a result, bellhops gladly run errands for her. The concierge arranges for a limousine if Becker wants to go out at night. Hotel restaurant waiters make certain that she never has to wait for a seat, since Becker has made it clear she cannot tolerate room service food.

"'I go to the drug store and pick up her prescriptions,' said bellhop James Casey, 75, who has worked at the Biltmore for 43 years. 'During the remodeling construction, I got bottled water for her.'

"'These are my friends,' Becker said of the maids, bellhops and desk clerks. 'This is my family.'

"So Becker was anxious when she learned this week that a new management company had been named to run the 65-year-old hotel, which is owned by a group of investors.

"On Wednesday, she sought assurances that the Millennium Biltmore's 600 employees' jobs were secure and that the downtown landmark would continue to be run as if it were home."

Thelma Becker died March 8th, 2004, fifty-three years after first checking into the Millennium Biltmore. She was 90 years old. "She had a lot of personality and was fun-loving, very talkative and her no-nonsense manner was refreshing." Holly Barnhill, formerly a publicist at the Millennium Biltmore, told the *Los Angeles Times*.

"Thelma Becker, a businesswoman who checked into the Millennium Biltmore Hotel in downtown Los Angeles in 1940 and checked out 53 years later, has died. She was 90," the *Times* said.

"Becker died at Kaiser Permanente Hospital in Los Angeles of natural causes, said her friend, Holly Barnhill. Becker, who had been in failing health in recent years had been living in a nursing home.

"As an assistant sales manager for Barbizon lingerie in the early 1940s, Becker pioneered the career woman's lifestyle, traveling regularly and meeting with buyers in the downtown Los Angeles retail and garment districts. The hotel at 5th Street and Grand Avenue was convenient for her work.

"Through the 1950s she was one of a number of full-time residents at the hotel who stayed in small rooms with a Murphy bed and a tiny closet. Over the years she got to know all the employees, some of whom thought of her as family.

Becker's living arrangement attracted attention to both her and the hotel. Newspaper articles about her led guests to look her up. Some of them had their picture taken with her and kept in touch by letter. She was a prolific correspondent.

Occasionally, she led tours through the historic building, pointing out the Crystal Ballroom where the Academy Award Oscar statuette was designed on a hotel napkin during a Hollywood gathering in 1927, and naming the famous guests, including the Beatles and President John F. Kennedy.

The organizers of the Olympic Games stayed at the Millennium Biltmore in 1984 when the Summer Games were held in Los Angeles. "There were six security people on every floor," Becker said in a 1988 interview. "I never felt so safe."

New employees at the Millennium Biltmore were introduced to Becker as part of their orientation. She lived in a tiny room near the elevator on the fifth floor. It was cluttered with photographs and several rolling racks for clothes that didn't fit into her closet.

"Several different managers wanted to move Thelma to a bigger room," said Millennium Biltmore chauffeur Joe Gedeon in an interview with *The Times*. "She didn't want it; she liked the one she *had*."

Daniel Day Lewis, in his portrayal of Abraham Lincoln, had nothing on George Billings who starred in a silent movie of the iconic American president. As recounted in a news article of the time:

> "Great excitement reigned among the attaches of the Hotel Biltmore when George Billings, screen actor, walked into the lobby.
>
> "Billings, it will be recalled, gained fame by his portrayal of the title role in the big silent film *Abraham Lincoln*. The critics at the time of the release lavished paragraphs upon his resemblance to the martyred President, and the similarity is noticeable off the screen.
>
> "Indeed, Billings, who has been at the Biltmore prior to filming, encouraged the resemblance by wearing clothes patterned after those affected by the great Lincoln and suiting his stride to a long, loose lope that, the historians tell us, served to get his prototype over the ground when he was in the throes of debate with Douglas.
>
> "Clad in true Lincoln raiment and looking like nothing in the world but a photograph of Lincoln suddenly come to life, Billings strode into the Millennium Biltmore today. The bellboys and the doorman, whose livery is gray, turned a shade paler than their uniforms, and the bellhops deserted their bench en masse to take to the shadowy depths behind the desk.
>
> "'Here, here,' stormed the head clerk, turning to the deserters. 'What's the idea running out on your posts like this?'
>
> 'That guy—' pointing to Billings, 'that's Lincoln, ain't it?' ex-

plained one of the boys when he had mastered his chattering teeth sufficiently to make himself heard. 'Well, we ain't gonna let him catch us in these gray uniforms. Suppose he mistook us for Confederate soldiers?'

"'That isn't Lincoln,' the clerk stated. That's Billings, who plays Lincoln on the screen.'

"'Well,' observed a guest who was standing by the desk, turning to get a view of the actor, 'he seems to think he's Lincoln. And I'll bet he won't be happy till he gets assassinated!'"

Ronald Reagan, who was fêted at the Millennium Biltmore just before he moved into The White House, always maintained an uncanny equilibrium during even the toughest cross examination by the press and political opponents. It was reminiscent of FDR's composure during the early years of World War II. In Bob Schieffer's book *America*, the TV news correspondent talks about Reagan's ability to disarm critics by poking fun at himself. "When he was accused of being distracted, Reagan told visitors to the Oval Office," Schieffer writes, "'someday they will say Ronald Reagan slept here.'" This was also a reference as well to the George S. Kaufman and Moss Hart play *George Washington Slept Here*. Reagan had attended a number of other major events at the Millennium Biltmore including the Academy Awards. His photo hangs prominently in the hotel along with other stars and dignitaries. After leaving The White House Reagan and his wife Nancy lived in the Bel Air section of Los Angeles. Much heralded cabaret singer Chris Barrett remembers the former President coming to the Bel Air Hotel to hear Chris sing and play Broadway show tunes. "He usually came by himself with some Secret Service people and had a smile for everyone."

Cary Grant enjoyed supporting the Variety Boys and Girls Club. The 1st annual Gala of the Variety Boys and Girls Club was held at the Millennium Biltmore Hotel. The Variety Club was founded back in 1949. The Variety Club, according to the Club's website, is "an international organization of people in the entertainment industry whose goal it is to help under-privileged children."

Rudolph Valentino and hundreds of other stars twinkled and shined at the Millennium Biltmore.

Rudolph Valentino and on and off-screen lover Pola Negri, one of the most beautiful of all film stars, arrived at the Millennium Biltmore in 1923. He died in August 1926, just a little while after Valentino, he who was married to Natasha Rambova, came to the Millennium Biltmore with Negri.

The Sixty Club gave an exclusive party for them at the Millennium Biltmore. But earlier in the day, Valentino narrowly escaped serious injury in a car crash.

"While many dashing costumes enlivened the Sixty Club party that night at the Millennium Biltmore, attention was lavished on the dashing Spanish creations worn by Pola Negri and Rudolph Valentino.

"Though Rudolph Valentino's car dashed from the coast highway about ten miles north of San Luis Obispo the prior morning the star and his three male companions escaped serious injury. The accident occurred immediately after the Isotta-Franchini automobile roared through San Marguerita and as the star attempted to take a turn at a too rapid rate. The machine dashed across an open stretch of country after leaving the highway, careened over the Southern Pacific roadbed and rails, wrecking a telephone pole and a crossing signal in its path."

An old news article on ClassicGlamourChic.com summed up some of Valentino and Negri's amorous adventures this way:

"Pola, who had, of course been invited to the party, took one look at this strange phenomenon, and turned the exclusive and delightful little evening into a Fourth of July celebration.

"Whether or not Pola actually slapped Rudy's face or boxed his ears in the very presence of his friend from overseas, I don't know. I shouldn't like to pretend that I did. One never does know, in a case like that, even if one has seen it with one's own eyes.

"Be that as it may, the Pola-and-Rudy affair was distinctly off-again from that time forth and until Lady Loughborough, having seen a great deal more of Hollywood than most people ever see, went back to her home and her husband in England.

"The things Pola said about Rudy—Pola is so descriptive!

"It amounts almost to a gift.

"It was rumored when Rudy went down to the Arizona desert for a movie location trip that a tent would be pitched for Pola too. That she would be his guest.

"Perhaps some level-headed friend convinced Pola that she didn't have any 'oil interests' which needed looking after on the desert.

"Anyway, the tent was never pitched for Pola.

"But in no time at all it was on-again, and Pola took back everything, with her irresistible smile, and said that Rudy was the great love of her life, and she must love somebody and Rudy was quite the most satisfactory sweetheart she had found in America. And that is covering a lot of territory.

"When they are on again, they really are quite entrancing, Pola and Rudy. When they do the tango together, they give you chills up and down your spine, which is the correct place for them, as you can ascertain by reading Mme. Elinor Glyn's stories.

"You do not really know whether they are dancing it very well or whether they are dancing it rather badly.

"You only know that they look quite mad about each other, and people ought to be quite mad about each other to dance the tango. That is, I would say, really the only excuse for dancing the tango at all.

"But still, though Pola forgave Rudy for his very polite attentions to Lady Loughborough and consented to put back on the gorgeous solitaire that almost covers her entire hand, and though Rudy forgave Pola for boxing his ears—or was it slapping his face or what have you—things do look a little precarious.

"For now when Pola goes to call upon Rudy, or to dine with him, or to attend a party, though she doesn't take any mad money or carry roller-skates under her arm, she does leave her limousine waiting very handily at the door.

No longer does she send it away and tell the driver when to call for her.

It is all most upsetting. A man cannot settle down to his work, never knowing how this thing is progressing. I am not given to exaggeration, but in a manner of speaking it is trying to the digestion not to know whether you are going to be scooped on a Pola and Rudy's secret wedding in a bower of orchids, or whether somebody is going to find Rudy or Pola with a stiletto in his or her back, just after the magazine has gone to press.

"If no more ladies from England invade Hollywood, all may be well. And I hope they won't.

"And I do hope dear Pola and dear Rudy will stop this off-again, on-again stuff now that Lady Loughborough is gone again, and make it "fine-again" one way or the other."

(For those readers who simply can't get enough of Rudy V, and of ClassicGlamourChic, I have included another amusing Valentino tidbit in the appendices—an article allegedly written by the Sheik himself explaining just how trying, and unfair, it is to be a beloved world-famous movie star.)

Film star Marion Davies, girlfriend of newspaper czar William Randolph Hearst (yes, the same Hearst infamously characterized by Orson Welles in *Citizen Kane*), was a frequent guest at the hotel. The Marion Davies Foundation Benefit was held in the Biltmore Bowl on June 25, 1934. Davies and Hearst were rumoured to have had one child, the late Patricia Lake, who was born in the 1920s and whom both Hearst and Davies spent time with when she was growing up. Lake was known as Davies' niece.

Even some household names performed a number of very domestic or "household" feats at the Millennium Biltmore. Jascha Heifetz, world-famous violinist, showed his talent for cooking at the Millennium Biltmore.

"When is an egg not an egg? When it's an omelet!" the *Los Angeles Times* reported.

"'When is an omelet not an omelet? When it's a creation, when it has soul, when I, Jascha Heifetz, make it!'

"Jascha Heifetz, world famous violinist, stood in the kitchen of the Biltmore Hotel yesterday morning, with two eggs in his vest pockets and a hot frying pan in his left hand.

"A creative frenzy was upon him. He was about to put soul in an omelet. It seems that his is a genius nourished upon omelet, that omelet is as necessary to this genius as a violin; but that only Omelet Heifetz has the desired inspirational effect.

"Certain songs must be sung to the omelet at certain times, incantations accompany the pinch of salt and piece of butter. So mysterious is the magic art of constructing the omelet, bringing it to life, giving it soul, that chefs the world over have given up in despair all efforts to imitate it, declared the musician.

"Therefore, Heifetz cooks his own. This is how he did it yesterday.

"Took about a dozen eggs; shook each one and held it up to light; selected two and placed in vest pockets.

"Grasped frying pan with banjo or violin grip and while lump of butter melted did fingering exercises on handle.

"Broke two eggs into frying pan, quickly added two tablespoons of cream, beat wildly, doing fox trot steps at same time. Closed eyes and added seasoning with appropriate incantations.

"'The omelet requires five minutes to cook and during the process one must visualize it in its finished perfection,' he stated. 'One must project one's soul into it.'

"Chef Mathieu of the Millennium Biltmore declared yesterday upon the conclusion of the Heifetz omelet demonstration that an omelet is never more than an omelet and has accepted the famous violinist's challenge to produce one just as good without the aid of magic. The contest will be a feature of the next Olympic Games."

But the Millennium Biltmore didn't just attract the stars. It also made many.

"Traffic Officer C. H. Cleaves was graduated yesterday from his post of North Broadway out by the railway yards to—and note the contrast

—the corner of Fifth and Olive Streets by the Biltmore and the Philharmonic," the *Los Angeles Times* reported in an article called "The Smiling Policeman."

"He is the cop (as all North Broadway motorists know) who bows and touches his hat and smiles most lovingly at every motorist that passes and as many pedestrians as he can sandwich in.

"Cleaves' first day in the high-toned district was a sensation. To have a traffic officer smile and touch his hat and gesture as if to say, like a head waiter, 'Will you please go ahead, sir?' was too much for the sophisticated. They thought it had something to do with April 1. Angelinos who had never seen Cleaves work and tourists from wide and far stood on the curbs and stared. Cleaves had 'em grinning with him for blocks around.

"One man stalled his engine so astonished was he (he drove a Ford) at the honor implied in the policeman's salute, and jaywalkers, caught red-handed, turned pale when they were requested, most apologetically, to retrace their steps.

"Policeman Cleaves was going fine and was getting in strong with the Biltmore patronage until one of his old North Broadway patrons drove his delivery wagon past and yelled, 'Hey, Happy, your shirt tail's hangin' out.' This North Broadway comedy was a great shock to the Fifth Street patronage, but Happy the Cop did not become ritzy with his old friend, yet his salute was not so cordial, it seemed.

"Policeman Cleaves says he gets better results by his methods and in the end less work. And, anyway, it's all in a day's work and why not pass happiness on and a smile is better than a frown and do unto others as you would have them do unto you.

"But get this right, folks. 'Happy' Cleaves will throw you into jail just as quick as that cop down at Seventh and Broadway, whose face looks as if he was always eating lemon drops."

Then there's the "Masquerade of the Princess" who stayed at the Millennium Biltmore in quest of stardom. "Another royal title launched on the uncertain seas of publicity vanished like a bursting bubble last night when 'Princess Beatriz De Ortega Braganza, of Alhambra, Granada, Spain, scion of four houses of royal blood,' faded from the horizon of Hollywood moviedom and Los Angeles society and became plain Miss Beatriz De Ortega, 1259 O'Farrell Street, San Francisco."

Nor should we ever forget the story of Mrs. Mary Rose Bell, a member of the Nadeau family whose house once stood on the site of the Millennium Biltmore. And did she love to dance! I'll bet she found the Crystal Ballroom at the Millennium Biltmore more accommodating for dancing than her old living room.

As with any long-lived, great hotel there have been through the years a plethora of offbeat events. No volume could do them all justice but I will entertain you with a couple of my faves:

The 3rd Annual Witchcraft and Sorcery Convention in 1973. Its guest of honor was science fiction superstar Ray Bradbury. Guests included:

JOHN AGAR—star of many science fiction (i.e., *Tarantula*) and fantasy films. Agar was once married to Shirley Temple.

KIRK ALYN—"Superman" in first serial. Also appeared in *Blackhawk* film.

BARRY ATWATER—the exciting "vampire-killer" in the movie *Night Stalker*.

ROBERT BLOCH—author of many fantasy stories and movie scripts. Noted for *Psycho* and *Asylum*.

RICH CORRELL—producer, actor, child star in *Leave It to Beaver* TV series. Other TV and movie roles.

BOB CLAMPETT—famous Warner Bros. (*Termite Terrace*) cartoon director who did *Beany and Cecil*. Also *Bugs Bunny, Porky Pig* and others.

DON GLUT—author of book on Frankenstein. Creator of the comic books "Dagar" and "Occult Files of Dr. Spektor."

D.C. FONTANA—head script writer of Star Trek series.

JUNE FORAY— actress, voice impressionist (Broom Hilda).

GEORGE CLAYTON JOHNSON—writer of premier episode of Star Trek. Co-author of *Logan's Run*. Author of many TV programs.

Bet you're all sorry you missed that one.

Then again, some events at the Millennium Biltmore have literally been for the birds:

"... At the Advertising Club's luncheon held at the Millennium Biltmore last Tuesday two of these feathered Lindberghs were released to carry a message of greeting to the Advertising Club of Honolulu," Guy Rowell reported in the *Los Angeles Times*.

"These birds have a flying radius of twenty-five hundred miles, and as it is about twenty-two hundred miles to Hawaii it is expected that their gas tanks will be pretty low when they arrive. Miss Mary Higgins, one of Charley Baad's guests at the Biltmore, released the pigeons from the structural platform built for the erection of the new addition to the big hotel."

Here are a few more press clippings of note, or at least notable activities, at the hotel:

> "The Los Angeles Biltmore continued to be an ad hoc Hall of Fame. Kingdon Gould, accompanied by his wife, was met by Jay Gould, Kingdon's brother. Kingdon is a fan [of the hotel, presumably] as far as his family is concerned."
>
> Jay Gould, you may or may not recall was one of the more famous railroad Robber Barons of the Gilded Age.

> "Marion Talley, the young opera singer that came out of the middle west and gave the blasé New Yorkers such a surprise last year, stayed at the hotel for some weeks."

> New York cabaret superstar Steve Ross told me, when I asked him his opinion of the Millennenium Biltmore on the west coast: "the hotel is very much my style."

"Miles Poindexter, Ambassador Extraordinary to Peru, was also a guest. He stressed the importance of good relations with our southern neighbors, and that possibilities for business down there are wonderful. There are many wealthy and aristocratic families who welcome our conveniences, our fashions, our moving pictures and our money, as capital is needed to develop the great natural resources of all South American countries."

Washington D.C. also spread its tentacles west to the Biltmore; a U.S. senate committee opened hearings on Boulder Dam at the Biltmore. The Reclamation and Irrigation Committee included Senators Hiram Johnson and Samuel Shortridge of California [among other notables].

The last word, as it so often does in Hollywood, must go to an agent:

In the 2013 play, I'll Eat You Last, *starring Bette Midler as super Hollywood agent Sue Mengers, Ms. Mengers talks about getting actress Faye Dunaway into* Chinatown, *costarring Jack Nicholson. A scene from the movie takes place at the Millennium Biltmore. One Mengerism, "Generally in Hollywood the more titles you have, the less important you are."*

6

Service at the Millennium Biltmore

"If you want great service, you have to have something great to serve." So says Joe Mills, Executive Sous Chef of the Millennium Biltmore, and he does! He even serves swiftly with a smile! You see, Mr. Mills is something of a kitchen athlete. I was fairly out-of-breath trying to tail him at one point.

The standards of service at the Millennium Biltmore were set originally by manager James Woods who worked at the New York Gilsey House, which is still standing, and the old Waldorf Astoria on 34th Street and Fifth Avenue. Today, General Manager Wanda Chan has put service first.

"To enhance the guests' experience, this is what we are here to deliver," Ms. Chan said in an interview for this book. "Guests may not remember exactly what you say, but they remember how you made them feel. We are here for the guests; we want them to be 'wow!' We want the first impression to be unforgettable."

"So we look after every detail for guests to understand we care." And she has plenty of help.

There's a classic song in *Les Miserables* called "Master of the House." And for me that description fits Steve Eberhard of the Millennium Biltmore to a "T". He's all that any hotel company could ever hope for in an employee. Hard working, easy to get along with, and loves his job. Steve's father also worked at the Millennium Biltmore.

Afternoon Tea

"Employees really make it happen day in and day out. A very big portion of our staff has over 20 years of service and many over 30 years, as well," Ms. Chan says.

The Millennium Biltmore service is without equal, considering its size. But size doesn't matter. For me, it's almost like a small hotel along the lines of one of my favorite small hotels, like the Casa Grandview in West Palm Beach where service is par excellence!

Smiles are what the Millennium Biltmore's restaurant "wait staff," room service waiters and bartenders have in spades and as a veteran grand hotel guest I can personally attest to this fact. The general manager of another grand hotel once told me, "If the server is gracious, that's the ideal." Along with bringing a guest what they ordered!

Not only did the Millennium Biltmore become the first grand hotel in Los Angeles, it significantly influenced the hotels that followed. When the Beverly Wilshire was built, its backers swarmed all over the Millennium Biltmore to see what if anything they could include that the Millennium Biltmore had but they hadn't counted on.

"Long-time employees have served as food and beverage directors and general managers, and our job as managers is how you keep it fresh, how you keep it exciting," Ms. Chan says.

"The hotel business is a people business. You need to keep people motivated and concentrate on guests," one executive said. "I came through the ranks. I've been the dishwasher, I've been the bartender, I have been the bar manager, the chef, the restaurant manager. Any time you're dealing with a large number of guests, in particular with banquet rooms and so forth, you have every single person sitting at these events as a potential return client, a consumer."

"A lot of people take it for granted the importance of having a really good banquet service team and banquet culinary team. But every single event is its own event," according to one executive.

"We are here to produce memorable experiences for the guest," says Ms. Chan. "We care that everything is thoughtfully planned for the guests' enjoyment. It all goes back to the people we select for the hotel. We really believe in hiring the right people for the right job. The 'right people' means people with the right attitude. You can teach people the right process, how to do this, step one-two-three. What you cannot teach people is to be nice and to genuinely care about pleasing the guest and making the guest happy. So finding the right people and keeping them

Gallery Bar

motivated and excited about service is important. You have to want to mentor people.

"This hotel is home away from home for the guest—especially the guest who travels for business. Or if they are by themselves and they don't want to go out to eat, room service is very important.

"It is to them a luxury. For guests who travel for business, room service is a luxury. Room service is not an afterthought. Room service truly reflects the quality of the hotel. So we pay a lot of attention to room service."

"In a recent letter to staff and guests marking the 90th Anniversary, General Manager Wanda Chan encapsulated her working philosophy and her feelings about the hotel's past, present and future:

"Throughout the last 90 years as hotelier and service professionals, the Biltmore hotel staff has carried on a tradition and a service culture, has become experienced in welcoming guests from near and far, working in every kind of occasion and situation. Nurturing and evolving the spirit of hospitality requires people who care, who work hard in delivering the service one would expect from the Biltmore, and in exceeding guest expectations. I have the privilege to work with an amazing group of staff; you are talented, and you are passionate about service. We work together to find ways to make a difference, and we help each other to learn and grow. Remarkable as it may seem, twelve employees observing *25-plus years with the Biltmore* celebrate their anniversaries in this milestone month of October. Congratulations to all and we thank you for your dedicated service!

"Growing older as a person and as a company is a privilege. The privilege of achieving yet another year in business. As we celebrate the past, we take time to reflect on the 90-year journey of the Biltmore. Our service culture is as relevant today as it was in the past. Millennium Hotels and Resorts gives us real clarity and real conviction for what we want the brand to stand for and what we are committed to bringing to our customers. Our highest priority is to treat both guest and employee with the utmost care and concern. Our primary goal is to provide our guests with a quality experience that is indicative of

Club Level Suite

the Millennium promise and to be a model of excellence as a leader in hospitality.

"We are honored to have Office of the Mayor, City of Los Angeles presenting Millennium Biltmore Hotel with the proclamation signed by Mayor Eric Garcetti, Council President Herb Wesson Jr., Jose Huizar and all Council members. The Resolution is now proudly displayed in our Sales and Catering Office.

"We are proud to accept the challenge of serving and the challenge of competing in an ever changing market. All that we have lived through and achieved in the past has equipped us to engage this challenge. The wisdom, skills, and love for people that characterizes us are needed to meet the challenges and carry forth to the future and the next generation. In this light, let's be inspired by new insights and continue on our journey. As a team, we will continue to transform this great hotel and make it relevant. Thank you all for your continued support."

Biltmore Bowl

"I interview all new (potential) staff in the Rendezvous Court, the hotel's former lobby, because I want them to feel awe-inspired by this grand hotel," Steve Eberhard explains. By the way, he is also a second generation Millennium Biltmore Hotel employee. "I'm going to ask a little more from my team. Here, the staff have to be comfortable interacting with guests, asking them, 'What may I get you?' or sense when a guest is in need of something. If they are not comfortable with that level of commitment they will not fit in well here."

A major part of service in any hotel is offering things that are worthy of being served superbly. Such is the case with Shakespeare. And it takes exceptional actors to do the Bard the justice he so richly deserves. So it is with the Millennium Biltmore. But having a great vehicle, you also need a great director. The Millennium Biltmore has always had these in spades. Take Baron Long, blessed with great spaces but buffeted by the Great Depression.

"One of the secrets of Baron Long's success at the Millennium Biltmore was his transformation of the Sala de Oro ballroom, located off the South Galeria, into the world's largest night club, which he christened the Biltmore Bowl," Margaret Leslie Davis writes in *Host of the Coast*. "Wayne McAlister, the architect, made sure that all seats, fanning out on five levels, commanded perfect views. On opening night on April 5, 1934, a $5 admission ticket paid for a bottle of French champagne and the continuous entertainment of Hal Roberts and his orchestra."

Under Long's stewardship the 1,400-foot-long Bowl became Los Angeles's preeminent entertainment venue. Music lovers, movie stars, and the city's social set flocked to the hotel to dine and dance to such Big Band headliners as Harry James and Jimmy Grier. When the 1939 Academy Awards ceremony was held at the Biltmore Bowl, more than 1,200 guests watched Bette Davis receive an Oscar for *Jezebel* and Spencer Tracy accept his for *Boys Town*. The renowned director Frank Capra was honored for the best picture of the year, *You Can't Take It with You*.

The Bowl was remodeled in the 1950s to add the Regency Room, a 16,800-square-foot exhibit hall located directly below it. In 1976 concert scenes from *A Star Is Born*, starring Barbra Streisand and Kris Kristofferson, were filmed inside the Bowl. One of the premier nightspots in the country during its glory years in the 1930s and 1940s, the Biltmore Bowl played host to the top social events in Los Angeles.

In fact, as soon as it opened, in 1934, the Biltmore Bowl became the city's most popular attraction and gave a lift to hotel revenues. With its lavishly ornamented ceiling and arched colonnades, the Bowl repeated the hotel's Renaissance architectural themes. Under Baron Long's management, even the staff was able to party in the Bowl during an annual employees-only event featuring the Big Band sounds.

7

Chairman Kwek, the Globe-Trekking Businessman Bringing the Millennium Biltmore into the Third Millennium

Millennium & Copthorne Hotels plc (M&C), listed on the London Stock Exchange since 1996, is a dynamic, global hotel company which owns, asset manages and/or operates a worldwide portfolio of over 100 hotels across seven distinct global brands—Grand Millennium, Millennium, Grand Copthorne, Copthorne, M Hotel, Studio M and Kingsgate—throughout Asia Pacific, Europe, Middle East, and North America.

Millennium Hotels and Resorts (MHR) was established as a global brand by Millennium & Copthorne Hotels plc to provide a common marketing and operating platform across its entire portfolio. Founded on the philosophy of genuine hospitality, this dynamic hospitality group has an outstanding reputation for excellence, taking pride in exceeding the needs of its business and leisure travelers. The strategic locality of its properties in gateway cities such as London, Paris, Dubai, Abu Dhabi, Doha, Singapore, Beijing, Shanghai, Seoul, Taipei, Hong Kong, Kuala Lumpur, and Bangkok makes MHR the perfect address to conduct your business or indulge yourself while on holiday.

Established in the United States in 2000, the North American arm of MHR includes a portfolio of 14 hotels in New York, Los Angeles,

Chicago, Boston, Anchorage, Boulder, Buffalo, Cincinnati, Durham, Minneapolis, Nashville, Scottsdale, and St. Louis.

That's the corporate boiler plate, but the man behind the company letterhead is a charming and worldly fellow by the name of Chairman Kwek. The Chairman has had tremendous success owning and renovating historic properties. He combines the best qualities of a real estate magnate, including understanding when to buy and sell properties, and relates to Conrad Hilton's passion for hotels. He has the controlling interest in more than 100 Millennium hotel properties around the globe. As for preserving landmark properties, he is almost without equal. Next door to and now part of the Chairman's Millennium Broadway Hotel complex on 44th St. is the Hudson Theatre, the oldest theater on Broadway above 42nd St., which was painstakingly restored, at great expense and with great attention to historic detail. So, too, with the Knickerbocker in Chicago. Had Chairman Kwek bought the Millennium Biltmore earlier, he might have saved the Biltmore Theatre which was razed in 1967.

The Chairman's strategy in acquiring the Millennium Biltmore in Los Angeles is all wrapped up in his current global strategy for many such large and historic hotels all across the world. You see, no one knows better than the Chairman just how the hotel business is being revolutionized in the third millennium. You can't just open the doors of a hotel as large as the Millennium Biltmore and expect it to fill up with customers as one did in the old days when people pulled into town in a train and headed for the nearest accommodations. Today people fly and they drive and some of them even travel about in helicopters. A large modern hotel in a large metropolis has to modernize, has to adjust to its clients' new needs.

Take for example the Millennium Biltmore's recent extensive renovations. Which does two things: it brings other types of business into the property and also brings the property to a size which is more manageable for attracting clients. The challenge of the hotel's plan is to fill it with customers who appreciate the value of it. With the dramatic improvement of downtown L.A. it's only logical that it would continue to go that way. Consider the importance of the hotel's downtown location, near such historic areas as Pershing Square, just opposite the hotel. Hotel people have realized you've got to have the green areas in downtown.

Had the Chairman purchased the Millennium Biltmore a number of years earlier, he might even have renovated the Biltmore Theatre the way he did the Hudson Theatre in New York.

Being an hotelier is a very complicated business, and even more so nowadays. There's a lot more to it than good room service and prompt wake-up calls.

Chairman Kwek spends two-thirds of each year in Singapore where he was born and raised and where his Hong Leong Group is now headquartered. The other third of the time he spends playing an active role in the asset management of his vast hotel and other holdings around the globe. He views himself as a real estate developer first and an hotelier second, and learned much about real estate from his late father.

"My father came from China originally," he said. "He started as a building supplier and he went into real estate, not as a developer. His first love was real estate. I took over the chairmanship of Hong Leong Group in 1990, although I had been actively leading several companies within the group before that." (Millennium and Copthorne Hotels PLC is a subsidiary of the Hong Leong Group Singapore.)

The Chairman, ever practical, talked about his group of hotels including the historic Millennium Biltmore Hotel Los Angeles where the Academy Awards ceremonies were once held. "I'm not trying to lead hotel chains. I can't have a critical number like Starwood or Intercontinental; I just can't do that. But I, unlike the hotel people, I have a lot of real estate experience. With the Millennium Biltmore Hotel I'm converting some of the offices within the Millennium Biltmore, and altogether I'm converting some 200 rooms into condominiums."

Chairman Kwek explained he was a real maverick in the hotel business. "I'm a contrarian in the sense that many hotel companies want to get all the management contracts they can, around the world. My approach to hotels is not only management but real estate. I have an extra strategy. With many of my hotels like the Millennium Biltmore we can eventually convert them into condominiums."

"They have another life," I interjected.

"They have another life," he said. "So what we want to do now is seriously look at some of our hotels, to reposition them, bringing some of the hotels to a much higher standard. In fact I have a designer doing a prototype design of the rooms for me in Singapore. The design is "East Meets West." It's a fusion between East and West because I strongly believe that, you know, Chinese travel will become the dominant traveling force in years to come. In four or five years, they will be the greatest travelers. And I want them—it's not exactly Asian design—to feel that they are at home. The luxury of the West, and the touch of the East."

In fact, a number of rooms at the Millennium Biltmore have been designed this way. "The Biltmore, I think, was an 880-room hotel," he said. "The previous owner converted 250 rooms into offices. We're converting back office space into condominiums, because downtown Los Angeles now is getting very popular. People living in L.A. have found that they have to drive for two to three hours every morning in traffic jams, before they can come downtown. So the condominium prices there are very good now. And it is convenient to have condominiums inside the hotel providing the hotel services to the condominiums. This is quite fashionable now." Specifically, The Chairman told me in March 2014 that, "We intend to convert two floors at the Biltmore Court [office tower] into 'extended-stay' apartments comprising 19 units per floor." The 25-story Biltmore Court, completed in 1987, is where the Biltmore Theatre had stood.

The Chairman also said that in the last several months, "Millennium & Copthorne has announced three hotel acquisitions to boost its global presence. Completion of these acquisitions is expected in the first half of 2014." These include:

• A hotel located within the Chelsea Harbour district in London believed to be the City's only five-star luxury all-suite hotel. It is currently operating as the Wyndham Grand London Chelsea Harbour and offers 154 suites and four penthouses, situated on the prestigious River Thames and is part of the Chelsea Harbour development. Originally it was a Conrad Hilton.

• A 480-room 4-star Novotel New York Times Square located in the heart of Manhattan theatre district. This newly refurbished hotel is in Times Square where on each New Year's eve, the ball drops at mid-night.

• The 5-star Boscolo Palace Roma hotel in Rome, Italy. Situated on Via Veneto, one of the city's most attractive streets, the hotel offers 87 luxury guest rooms and suites, and is well located to serve the needs of visitors to Vatican City. "Rome is one of the most popular tourist destinations in the world. This acquisition adds an important new destination to Millennium & Copthorne's European portfolio. Millennium & Copthorne has been seeking to establish a presence in Rome for many years, and this acquisition continues its strategy of selective growth through careful investment in gateway cities," the Chairman said.

I have gotten to know the Chairman fairly well in recent years. He and I, you see, share a passion for luxury hotels. He for building, buying and renovating them, and me for staying at them. Well, it takes two to tango, you know. However, most big businessmen these days rarely have time to waste on little people like hotel-book writers. There again, the Chairman doesn't fit the mold. He has been more than generous with me with his time and his theories about modern hotel management. When I was researching my book on London's Grand Hotels, I got to spend some real quality time with the Chairman. In fact, I'd like to quote a passage from that book because I think it is the best way to give you a good overall impression of the man himself and his thinking about what to do with great hotels of the past as we all move further into the digital age:

It was a little like lounging around in one of your fondest, and wildest, dreams. Not too long ago, in real life, I was astonished to find myself sitting in the rounded living room in the Millennium Hotel Paris, looking out at the busy Boulevard Haussman and the pinnacle of the Paris Opera House. Part of me can sense the Germans approaching Paris in the movie fiction of *Casablanca*; another part of me: Hemingway's *A Moveable Feast*, his views of Paris are the epitome of literature, music, art and just plain life.

Here shortly after writing *Life at the Top: Inside New York's Grand Hotels*, I'm planning another book about hotels and can't help but marvel at Chairman Kwek's far-flung hotel empire, at once modern and sleek, and alternately historic and grand, brimming with the best of the past blending with the best of the present and future. Four months earlier I sat in London with the Chairman, the owner of this and many other hotels including Broadway's Millennium and its Hudson Theatre.

The Mayfair Millennium is one of several hotels Millennium owns in London. Another of the Chairman's London properties is Bailey's, a traditional and historic hotel built in 1876 which is near Kensington Gardens, Hyde Park and the National History Museum. It's right by the Gloucester Hotel in Kensington, which is also a Millennium Hotel.

I sat with Chairman Kwek (referred to by his colleagues as 'the Chairman') one late fall afternoon in the posh restaurant of his Millennium Knightsbridge Hotel in the heart of London's fashionable Sloane Street shopping district. Our conversation ranged from Gucci, Fendi and other shops in the area to the hotel 'across the pond' in New York City with its Hudson Theatre.

"This hotel was a Holiday Inn a long time ago," he said, referring to the hotel we were in at the moment, as we tasted a special noodle dish. "They had a swimming pool on this level, and then somebody from South Africa took it over. Then during the recession American Express offered me this deal. And I redecorated the lobby and exterior. ..."

The Chairman once took Steve Wynn to the Bombay Brasserie, an Indian restaurant which has made a name for itself as a favorite of celebrities, next to Bailey's Hotel. "Was he considering becoming a partner?" I ask. "No, no. He was here, at that time, when London was supposed to be—England was supposed to be—opening up to international casino operators and owners, so he was looking at London, and I happened to be here. I've known him a year. So we talked and I took him to see the Bailey's Hotel. He liked the Bombay Brasserie which he said he could see putting in Las Vegas."

Conversation moved to The New York Plaza Hotel which Chairman Kwek had sold with Prince Alwaleed in 2005. "I know the Prince spoke very highly of you when I talked to him for my Plaza book," I told him.

"He said that one of the reasons he got interested in The Plaza in the first place is that you were actually going to run the hotel."

The Chairman replied, "In fact, you know, when he wanted to sell The Plaza, his representative was telling me that he wanted to sell it for about five hundred million, so I thought he wanted to get out. I told him 'I will get out with you together, but leave it to me, I will sell it.'... So I actually managed to sell for close to seven hundred million.

"What happened was that, you know, the new owner sent his representatives to Singapore to talk with me and then we talked, I think, six hours or so. We agreed on basic terms and just shook hands because it was late and they flew back. And then within a week or so, the owner came over to London so I met up with him. We had lunch in Mayfair, and then we renegotiated. Elad Properties, the company which bought The Plaza, agreed to pay out employee compensation packages for a reduction of $25 million of the $700 million price negotiated thus far.

Hudson Theatre

"The Prince was so happy he invited me to Paris to talk with him so I went to his Georges V. He said that, 'Well, we have known each other now for almost ten years. This is the only project. We mustn't just say goodbye and then we'll continue to forge our relationship for the future—even strengthening it.' I say, 'Sure.' You know, in fact, I have no trouble with the Prince. He's a nice gentleman to work with."

And now back in London, our talk turned to Singapore and the Chairman's hopes for its artistic accomplishments as well as its business interests. "We are emphasizing now Singapore as a city where you'd like to live, like to work, want also to enjoy yourself," he explained. "That's why we are opening up the casino. The arts have also been a significant feature for the world-class city. Singapore is also an art center. Our Esplanade theater—looks like a porcupine you know—is iconic. So I certainly hope we can do something that is commercially viable. To present the best of Singapore in New York at the Hudson Theatre."

The Chairman and his team are considering a wide variety of options for the Hudson Theatre, he said, including concerts featuring Far Eastern artists and theater productions. "Singapore is promoting arts and culture, so I want to present some of these at the Hudson Theatre, inviting our best corporate clients, best travel agents," he said. "I know it may not be up to Broadway standards, but at least it's up to a standard that you feel a young country like Singapore can now achieve."

"Our New York hotels are now all doing well. They recently had a food festival, Asian food festival, in the Millennium U.N. Plaza. Our Chef Chan Kwok from our Singapore hotel has won the Chef of the Year in Asia. And our restaurant was Restaurant of the Year. I'm publishing a cookbook for him."

Harry Macklowe's innovativeness in building a state-of-the-art conference center in the hotel, coupled with Chairman Kwek's farsightedness in restoring the Hudson Theatre (which is sometimes used for major conferences as well as gala and theatrical events), has made the Millennium Broadway a powerful magnet for meetings, conventions and theatrical events.

"Basically, Harry did two very innovative things at the theater," explained a hotel employee who worked with the hotel and theater over a

13-year period. "One was the 'stepping down' of the seats, rather than traditional raked seating. He also added wonderfully comfortable seats for the theater, which were easily removable for a series of different events. But it took the innovativeness of Chairman Kwek to fully take advantage of that. Not only of the infrastructure but the restoration—bringing the theater back to its former grandeur. You can have a theater production in the evening and the next morning a presentation by a corporation."

"But it was really the Chairman's enthusiasm and support which have brought the Hudson to the wonderful condition it's in today," the employee concluded.

The renovation and restoration of the Hudson Theatre is very much in keeping with Chairman Kwek's overall vision and philosophy in running his hotel chain. It's essential to emphasize this as he is very mindful of the rich heritage of New York City, Broadway and most importantly, the Hudson Theatre itself. These were all key driving motivations for the Chairman in preserving the character of the theater. The Chairman has strong convictions that Broadway is unique to the world. Even though Broadway has undergone many transformations over the years, he believes in the vitality of New York City, in its captains such as Giuliani and Bloomberg, and in the resilience of its people and in the beauty of its location.

After discovering the history of the Hudson Theatre, the Chairman was honoured to be the owner of such a historical and important monument. He remains committed to ensuring the Hudson Theatre continues to shine together with the Millennium Hotels. He will continue to preserve the glory of the Hudson Theatre as a reminder of the culture of Broadway and its community. Or, as the Chairman says, "May the glory of the Hudson Theatre continue to flourish in the years to come."

Now you know a bit better why I have become such a fan of luxury hotels. In many ways, as the Chairman knows, they provide the last bastion of gracious living of a quieter, more elegant past as we all rush headlong into an unknown, chaotic future.

I think this account also provides some insight as to why the Chairman would be interested in a property like Los Angeles's Biltmore Hotel. L.A.'s grand old lady perfectly fits into the Chairman's notions about reconfiguring (financially, architecturally and culturally) the world capitals' great inns to serve the clients of a new, global economy. Grand hotels nowadays have to be like little United Nations, because business travelers now come from all over the world. A modern grand hotel not only has to accommodate these people, it must cater to their customs and tastes. As more and more the East meets West at the boardroom table, the great hotels in the great cities will play a crucial role, as ambassadors of good living.

8

Pershing Square and the Movie Palaces

"Before the Music Center rose in Bunker Hill, Los Angeles' cultural heart belonged to Pershing Square," the *Los Angeles Times* reported in 1997.

Pershing Square was first established in 1866 as the Los Angeles Town Square. By 1910, Los Angeles was small compared to many other U.S. cities, including Utica, New York, which was on the famous Barge Canal. L.A. was ranked 17th in population. Its population was just over 300,000.

D. W. Griffith started filming in L.A. with members of his actors company including Mary Pickford and Lionel Barrymore. In 1923, the year the Millennium Biltmore opened, Walt Disney, who would later be a regular at the hotel's Oscar and other ceremonies, arrived in L.A. with all of $40. The following year, 1924, the Los Angeles population reached one million; a year later the Los Angeles Central Library opened, and within the next two years Metro-Goldwyn-Mayer, Columbia Pictures, and Twentieth Century Fox put out their shingles.

The Millennium Biltmore spurred other hotel development in L.A. "The Beverly Wilshire was built because of the success of the Millennium Biltmore," Hank Elder, a Los Angeles real estate executive, said in an interview for this book.

Elder is with the firm of Grubb & Ellis which has been serving the Los Angeles County market since 1968. Grubb & Ellis serves this diverse market through its offices in Downtown Los Angeles, West Los Angeles, North Los Angeles, the South Bay and the San Gabriel Valley. The Los Angeles downtown office offers a full range of commercial real estate services.

Elder is also a long-time member of the old-guard Jonathan Club. The Jonathan Club also has a beach club where members play volleyball and paddle tennis. Members were overjoyed when news broke that a new Brooks Brothers store would be opening downtown as another sign of the beginning of a resurgence of downtown L.A.

The immediate area surrounding the Millennium Biltmore was like that around the Biltmore in New York (built in 1913) and the "new" Waldorf Astoria, built in 1931. An area populated by posh clubs and restaurants. The California Club was directly in back of the Los Angeles Biltmore; the old-guard Jonathan Club is still serving a well-established business clientele a stone's throw away.

In 1894 Pershing Square was a lush green oasis. "La Fiesta de Los Angeles" was held featuring the crowning of the queen of La Fiesta. It's now called "Fiesta Broadway." In 1910 the park was renovated by architect John Parkinson who designed the L.A. City Hall and Union Station. There's a monument to California's twenty Spanish-American War deaths, built in 1900 and thought to be one of the oldest public artworks in the city. Over the years the park has had constant renovations. Two features that have gotten widespread praise are the temporary winter ice skating rink and the dog walk areas. The corporation operating the Staples Center and L.A. Live complex is commissioning a plan to redesign and improve the park yet again as downtown has become a much more desirable place to live as well as work. As a long time resident of New York City, I was truly amazed by the convenience and cleanliness of the L.A. subway, with a station at the park which connects to many parts of the city.

Pershing Square, one square block in size, is bordered by 5th Street to the north, 6th Street to the south, Hill Street to the east, and Olive Street to the west.

"In the 1850s, the location was used as a camp by settlers outside of the Pueblo de Los Angeles, which was to the northeast around the

La Iglesia de Nuestra Senora Reina de los Angeles church, the plaza, and present day Olvera Street," according to Wikipedia. "1850s surveyors drew the site as ten individual plots of land, but in practicality it was a single 5-acre (20,000m) parcel. Canals distributing water from the Zanja Madre were adjacent. In 1866 the park site's block of plots was dedicated as a public square by Californio and new Mayor Cristobal Aguilar, and was first called *La Plaza Abaja*, or 'The Lower Plaza.' At some point the owner of a nearby beergarden, German immigrant George 'Roundhouse' Lehman, planted small native Monterey cypress trees, fruit trees, and flowering shrubs around the park, and maintained them until his death in 1882."

AEG, the corporation currently operating the Staples Center and L.A. Live complex is currently sponsoring a $700,000 redesign of Pershing Square. Efforts are currently underway to re-envision ways to improve the current park.

In the *Downtown Examiner* staff writer Aaron Downes interviewed famed photo journalist Gary Leonard about downtown L.A. during its down years:

"In the mid 70's [Downtown L.A.] was abandoned. After World War II they decided that freeways were the way. L.A. wasn't alone. You look at the sitcoms and that'll tell you what everyone was buying at large —living in the suburbs, driving on the freeways, all the zoning—so downtown was abandoned and no one was living down here. They had flop-houses and that was about the only people living here."

Of course many downtowns in large urban areas all over the country were going through this very same phenomenon of middle-class flight to the burbs during the Seventies. In lower Manhattan occurred the most famous of these events when city planner Robert Moses wanted to build a superhighway directly through Greenwich Village, razing historic buildings in a wide swath from the East River to the Hudson just so suburbanites on Long Island wouldn't have the inconvenience of driving through lower Manhattan neighborhoods on their way to visit suburbanites in New Jersey. A great, historic public outcry and uprising quashed those plans and urban planning took on a new crusader-like image that has lasted to the current day.

However, unlike New York not only did Los Angeles not cherish its architecture, it went one step further. At the prompting of the tire and auto companies (they were later convicted of racketeering and fraud) the city of Los Angeles shut down its entire rapid transit rail system. In some circles it was considered the most far reaching and efficient such system but no matter on June 1963 the last "red car" ran in Los Angeles. All 3200 miles of track was pulled up and the city was doomed to rely completely on the automobile. Interestingly today you can only see the red cars in the Disney classic *Who Framed Roger Rabbit* running down the streets of Los Angeles.

In Los Angeles, it was important downtown institutions like the Millennium Biltmore that took up the fight, for their own survival but also the survival of their beloved city.

"I'm on the executive committee of the CLA, so anything to promote downtown, bring business to downtown, we are 100 percent," explains Ms. Chan. "Pershing Square has cleared up a lot already but now through CLA we are actively promoting the renovation of the Convention Center which will help bring business to downtown."

During its early history, the Millennium Biltmore was practically bordered by the greatest concentration of movie palaces the world has ever seen. And if the Broadway Theater District in New York was—and is—the heart of legitimate theater in the United States, the Broadway Theater District in Los Angeles was the center of the cinema world.

"Stretching for six blocks from Third to Ninth Streets along South Broadway in Downtown Los Angeles, the district includes 12 movie theaters built between 1910 and 1931," according to Wikipedia.

By 1931, the district had the highest concentration of cinemas in the world, with seating capacity for more than 15,000 patrons. Broadway was the hub of LA.'s entertainment scene—a place where "screen goddesses and guys in fedoras rubbed elbows with Army nurses and aircraft pioneers."

In 2006, the *Los Angeles Times* wrote:

> *There was a time, long ago, when the streets of downtown Los An-*

geles were awash in neon — thanks to a confluence of movie theaters the world had never seen before. Dozens of theaters screened Hollywood's latest fare, played host to star-studded premiers and were filled nightly with thousands of moviegoers. In those days, before World War II, downtown L.A. was the movie capital of the world.

Los Angeles Times columnist Jack Smith called the neighborhood surrounding the Millennium Biltmore "the only large concentration of vintage movie theaters left in America."

I remember walking into those opulent interiors, surrounded by the glory of the Renaissance, or the age of Baroque, and spending two or three hours in the dream world of the movies. When I came out again the sky blazed; the heat bounded off the sidewalk, traffic sounds filled the street, I was back in the hard reality of the Depression.

So it's little wonder that the Millennium Biltmore on 5th Street was to become one of the original homes of the Oscar ceremonies.

In the years after World War II, the district began to decline as first-run movie-goers shifted to the movie palaces in Hollywood, in Westwood Village, and later to suburban multiplexes. After World War II, as Anglo moviegoers moved to the suburbs, many of the Broadway movie palaces became venues for Spanish-language movies and variety shows.

In 1988, the Los Angeles Times noted that, without the Hispanic community, "Broadway would be dead." Jack Smith wrote that Broadway had been "rescued and revitalized" by "the Latino renaissance."

The district has been the subject of preservation and restoration efforts since the 1980s. In 1987, the Los Angeles Conservancy started a program called "Last Remaining Seats" in which the old movie palaces were opened each summer to show classic Hollywood movies. In 1994, the Conservancy's associate director, Gregg Davidson, noted: "When we started this, the naysayers said no one will go downtown to an old theater to see an old movie in the middle of the summer, but we get a number of people who have never seen a movie in a theater with a balcony. The older people go for nostalgia. And the movie people—seeing a classic film on a big screen is a different experience."

After attending a Conservancy screening, one writer noted: "The other night I went to the movies and was transported to a world of powdered wigs and hoop skirts, a rococo fantasy of gilded cherubs and crystal chandeliers. And then the film started."

Despite preservation efforts, many of the theaters have been converted to other uses, including flea markets and churches. The Broadway movie palaces fell victim to a number of circumstances, including changing demographics and tastes, a downtown location that was perceived as dangerous at night, and high maintenance costs for aging facilities. With the closure of the Loew's State Theater in 1998, the Orpheum and the Palace were the only two still screening films.

In 2006, the *Los Angeles Times* wrote: "Of all of L.A.'s many hidden gems, maybe none is as sparkling nor as hidden as the Broadway theatre district downtown." Bemoaning the possible loss of such gems, the same writer noted: "L.A. gave birth to the movies. To lose the astonishing nurseries where the medium grew up would be tragic."

In 2008, the City of Los Angeles launched a $40-million campaign to revitalize the Broadway district, known as the "Bringing Back Broadway" campaign. Some Latino merchants in the district expressed concern that the campaign was an effort to spread the largely Anglo gentrification taking hold in other parts of downtown to an area that has become the city's leading Latino shopping district. A worker at one of the district's bridal shops noted, "on one side, I like the idea. The only thing is that I don't think they want our types of businesses."

9

Zeppelin (Graf not Led) Stops at the Millennium Biltmore, The Beatles Don't Fly In, and the Yogi Departs

Germany's Graf Zeppelin hovered over the Millennium Biltmore on a round-the-world jaunt in 1929 before landing at Mines Field (now L.A. Airport). As the crew and passengers banqueted at the hotel, the dirigibles' commissary was replenished with complete supplies from the kitchen.

The Graf Zeppelin made flights from Germany to North and South America but following the Hindenburg disaster in 1937, Zeppelin use was dramatically curtailed. On May 6, 1937, the Hindenburg caught fire as it came in for a landing, at Lakehurst Naval Air Station in New Jersey. The incident broke passengers' confidence in airships in general. Radio reporter Herbert Morrison, on the scene to talk about the first Zeppelin flight that year, reported the disaster which, along with Orson Welles' fictional account of Martians landing on Earth, has become one of the most famous and dramatic radio, or for that matter any, news accounts ever broadcast. Later airships, such as the ones used to advertise sports events today, would be filled with non-flammable helium and not hydrogen.

Of course, that's not the whole story. Back in the 30's America had a virtual monopoly on helium and was very reluctant to sell it to other nations, especially Germany. Whether this was prescience about the coming Nazi horde or simple xenophobia is difficult to tell. However, if the dirigible industry had taken flight in America as opposed to Germany, the Hindenburg disaster never would have happened and the far swifter and not much less elegant transatlantic crossing by balloon rather than steamship might have turned into a major industry. Of course, in only a few years, following in the flight path of Charles Lindbergh, the transatlantic airlines came into existence and the point became moot. It is true, however, that the early ocean-going airplanes could not compete with the spaciousness of a Graf Zeppelin. Such, however, are the winners and losers of history and of big business.

Many people forget now that the spire of the Empire State Building was originally designed as a mooring post for dirigibles. The zeppelins were supposed to float gracefully over the Manhattan skyline and deposit their well-fed passengers at the 114th floor of the Empire State Building, pulling into downtown as easily as the Twentieth Century Limited arrived at Grand Central Terminal from Chicago.

All this notwithstanding, back in 1929, the Millennium Biltmore's allure as a world-class destination was demonstrated dramatically when the German Graf Zeppelin hovered over the hotel on its round-the-world jaunt. The entire trip was sponsored by the news magnate William Randolph Hearst, and dailies from coast to coast reprinted the photograph of the dirigible soaring above the hotel's roof.

During their stopover in Los Angeles, the Graf's passengers and crew stayed at the Millennium Biltmore and its commissary was replenished with provisions from the hotel kitchen. Nine gourmet meals were packed in special containers that weighted nearly 2,500 pounds and included seven varieties of hors d'oeuvres, caviar, and pâté de foie gras.

The Millennium Biltmore even created souvenirs of the global event: nine sets of menus custom printed on engraved cards showing the dirigible floating in the sky above the hotel. In the 1930s new skyscrapers and civic monuments continued to rise around the hotel, as a 1936 postcard seductively showed.

Less fortuitously, it was also in the 1930s that the Los Angeles economy felt the bite of the Great Depression, and the Millennium Biltmore's once bustling atmosphere and strong profits slowed considerably. In December 1933 Baron Long, a local sportsman and hotel proprietor, assumed control of the landmark, beginning his family's thirty-six-year management of the Millennium Biltmore.

Confident that the depression was nearly over, Long declared that good times were returning to Los Angeles. "The Biltmore is one of the finest hotels in the world and I am proud to be at its head," he asserted. "We propose to make it the social and business hub of the entire Southland." Tall and impeccably dressed, Long settled into a desk in the hotel lobby, where he greeted guests personally and handled hotel business. His successor as the hotel's general manager was Edward S. Bernard, his close associate and adopted son.

Like any great, long-lived urban institution, various myths have sprouted up about the Millennium Biltmore. One of the more amusing is the story about the Beatles' first American tour in 1964. Everybody knows about the Fab Four getting mobbed at Idlewild Airport upon their arrival in New York in February. Everybody knows about their two appearances on the Ed Sullivan Show. Fewer people know about The Beatles' wild stay at The Plaza in New York, fewer still about their next concert stop in Washington, D.C. and then training down to Florida. Later that year in August they came back to the States for an extended American tour, beginning in San Francisco. When they got to Los Angeles a few days later a myth grew up about The Beatles being so mobbed that they had to be transported to the Millennium Biltmore's roof via helicopter. It's a great story, but, alas, there's no truth to it.

In fact, they didn't stay at a hotel in L.A. at all, but at a rented house at 356 St. Pierre Road in Brown Canyon, Bel Air. They did give the first of their three famous Hollywood Bowl concerts during that visit. George Martin, their Abbey Road and Parlophone producer, even came over to help Capitol Records make a live album of the concert. But even outdoors with the Bowl's great acoustics, the screaming of the fans was too raucous. It wasn't until 1977 that some of the songs from that event made it onto a Beatles record: The Beatles At the Hollywood Bowl.

It's probably a good thing they didn't stay at the Millennium Biltmore. Beatlemania was at such a fever pitch at that time that their fans might have dismantled the hotel piece by piece for souvenirs.

On March 19, 1952 the revered spiritual leader Paramhansa Yogananda transcended this earthly plain, suffering a heart attack at the age of 51 in the famous Crystal Ballroom of the Millennium Biltmore. While the official cause of his death was a heart attack his reverent follows believe he entered *mahasamadhi,* a sacred passing from one's mortal remains. While this may seem a macabre thing to bring up, in fact it is a joyous fact to his millions of followers that still teach and follow his spiritual foundations thru the Self-Realization Fellowships. During the year the Self-Realization fellowship holds a major convocation in downtown Los Angeles bringing adherents from all over the world to downtown Los Angeles. The other day I was speaking with one of Yogananda's followers and was told that the Biltmore is revered as a kind of "holy" pilgrimage within the sphere of the organization founded by the great yogi and philosopher.

As this member told me, "Many followers consider it a sacred privilege to experience the physical location of this most revered's last mortal moments on earth." The spot in the Biltmore is considered the place that Yogi experienced *mahasamadhi,* transmuting his consciousness from his body.

So the next time you are at the Biltmore find the spot and take a moment to wonder at the things that make the world a most remarkable place and those that lived remarkable lives within the hotel.

10

The Black Dahlia and the 1960 Democratic Convention—Furtive Doings at the Millennium Biltmore

Perhaps the most sensational crime story of the last century involved the Millennium Biltmore. Elizabeth Short, nicknamed "The Black Dahlia," was last seen at the Millennium Biltmore Bar. "The Black Dahlia" is sometimes confused with *The Blue Dahlia*, a 1946 film noir starring Alan Ladd and Veronica Lake. *Variety* said, "playing a discharged naval flyer returning home from the Pacific first to find his beautiful wife unfaithful, then to find her murdered and himself in hiding as the suspect, Alan Ladd does a bang up job. His performance has a warm appeal, while in his relentless track down of the real criminal, Ladd has a cold, steel-like quality that is potent. Fight scenes are stark and brutal and tremendously effective."

Critic Dennis Schwartz called the film, "a fresh smelling film noir directed with great skill by George Marshall from the screenplay of Raymond Chandler (the only one he ever wrote for the screen—his other films were adapted from novels of others and, ironically, habitations of his novels were all written by other screenwriters). It eschews moral judgment in favor of a hard-boiled tale that flaunts its flowery style as its way of swimming madly along in L.A.'s postwar boom and decadence periods"

"The Black Dahlia" was a nickname given to Elizabeth Short (July 29, 1924-January 15, 1947), an American woman who was the victim of a gruesome and much-publicized murder. Wikipedia says, "Short acquired the moniker posthumously by newspapers in the habit of nicknaming crimes they found particularly colorful. Short was found mutilated, her body sliced in half at the waist, on January 15, 1947, at Leimert Park, Los Angeles, California. Short's unsolved murder has been the source of widespread speculation, leading to many suspects, along with several books and film adaptations of the story. Short's murder is one of the oldest unsolved cases in Los Angeles history.

"In Florida, Short met Major Matthew Michael Gordon Jr., a decorated United States Army Air Forces officer who was assigned to the 2nd Air Commando Group and in training for deployment to China Burma India Theater of Operations. Short told friends that Gordon wrote her a letter from India, proposing marriage, while he was recovering from injuries sustained from an airplane crash. She accepted his proposal, but Gordon died in a second airplane crash on August 10, 1945, before he could return to the United States. She later exaggerated the story, saying that they were married and had a child who died. Although Gordon's friends in the air commandos confirmed that Gordon and Short were engaged, his family denied any connection after Short's murder.

"Elizabeth Short returned to Los Angeles in July 1946 to visit Army Air Force Lieutenant Joseph Gordon Fickling, an old boyfriend. They had met in Florida during the war. At the time Short returned to Los Angeles, Fickling was stationed at NARB, Long Beach. For the six months prior to her death, Short remained in Southern California, mainly in the Los Angeles area.

"The body of Elizabeth Short was found in the Leimert Park district of Los Angeles on January 15, 1947. The remains had been left on a vacant lot on the west side of South Norton Avenue midway between Coliseum Street and W. 39th Street.

"Due to the notoriety of the case, more than fifty men and women have confessed to the murder, and police are swamped with tips every time a newspaper mentions the case or a book or movie about it is released. Sergeant John P. St. John, a detective who worked the case until his retirement, stated, 'It is amazing how many people offer up a relative as the killer.'

"Gerry Ramlow, a *Los Angeles Daily News* reporter, later stated, 'If the murder was never solved it was because of the reporters. They were all over, trampling evidence, withholding information. It took several days for the police to take full control of the investigation, during which time reporters roamed freely throughout the department's offices, sat at officers' desks, and answered their phones. Many tips from the public were not passed on to police, as the reporters received them and then rushed out to get 'scoops.'"

"According to newspaper reports, shortly after the murder, Elizabeth Short received the nickname Black Dahlia at a Long Beach, California, drugstore in mid-1946 as wordplay on the then-current movie *The Blue Dahlia*. Los Angeles County district attorney investigators' reports state that the nickname was invented by newspaper reporters covering the murder. *Los Angeles Herald-Express* reporter Bevo Means, who interviewed Short's acquaintances at the drugstore, is credited with first using the Black Dahlia name."

Let us revisit the brief sad life of Elizabeth Short, whose last verified sighting pulled the Millennium Biltmore into the annals of romanticized crime. The third of five daughters, 6-year-old Elizabeth watched her Massachusetts family break apart when the Great Depression hit. No one could afford to build or patronize the miniature golf courses her father constructed. One day he drove off and all that was found was his abandoned car parked upon a bridge. Suicide was suspected. Not an easy determination for any of the Short survivors, especially a small girl with escalating asthma and bronchitis afflictions. She was shuttled back and forth between Florida winters and Massachusetts summers for her health, which seemed to instill wanderlust within her.

At age 19 she discovered her father, alive and well, and living in California working in a shipyard. She went there to live with him. From their San Francisco home they relocated to Los Angeles, but it seems this reunion was not a happy one. A fierce altercation split father and daughter with Elizabeth finding quarters first in Lompoc and then in Santa Barbara. It would appear that the combination of a broken home and unhappy father/daughter relationship affected her adolescent behavior, because she was soon arrested for underage drinking and was sent back to Massachusetts by California authorities. Medford would not suit her anchored wanderlust and Florida whispered to her to return. She did.

It would also appear that those shipyard days with her father spawned an attraction to fighting men with Elizabeth. Coupled with her introduction to early drinking, it doesn't seem hard to fathom that she would find company with military types. Once back in Florida, she got cozy with Major Matthew Michael Gordon, an officer in the United States Army Air Force. She claimed he sent her a marriage proposal from India while recovering from injuries due to an air crash. She claimed she accepted, but he died in a second crash before any nuptials developed. Friends say she later embellished this tale to include a marriage and a child who died. Gordon's friends verified that there was an engagement.

Short returned to L.A. in 1946 and spent time with an "old boyfriend" from Florida named Joseph Gordon Fickling, also with the AAF. She moved frequently within the Southern California area, but spent most of the time in or near L.A. If her relationship with Fickling ever blossomed, it was never noted.

She had been back in L.A. for about six months. She was last seen on January 9, 1947.

At 10 a.m. on January 15 of the same year, a passerby of Leimert Park glimpsed what she first thought to be a discarded mannequin. Closer inspection revealed it to be the body of Elizabeth Short, cut in half at the waist. Her mouth had been slashed open from each corner toward each ear, her body held cut marks upon her thighs and breasts, where chunks of flesh had been removed. Short's body had been washed, cleaned, and posed in a position with her arms over her head—at right angles—and her legs spread. Ligature marks were imbedded into her wrists, arms, and neck and there was bruising on the front and right side of her head with some small bleeding. The cause of death was hemorrhaging from the facial wounds and shock from the head trauma. The black tailored suit she was last seen wearing became part source for her tabloid identity: The Black Dahlia. The reference to the Mexican flower can only be speculated to have been blended from the title of the Alan Ladd—Veronica Lake starrer, although many stories abound about this moniker's origins.

It is the longest unsolved crime in Los Angeles' cold case files. In the wake of the crime, many people stepped forward to confess, but none were credible. Reporters crawled all over the crime scene and any spot where Short lived, played, shopped, or visited, in hopes of unearthing solid leads. There are those who held reporters responsible for the lack of a solution because of their zeal and trampling of areas holding evidence. It didn't take long for The Black Dahlia to move from the stuff of lurid squalor to the stuff of legends. And what aspect of this macabre murder drew in the prestigious Millennium Biltmore Hotel?

The last location Elizabeth Short and her smartly tailored black suit were seen was in the Millennium Biltmore Bar.

"The allures and romantic seductions of The Black Dahlia," mystery writer Douglas Allan Dean said to me, "are as numerous as the petals on that flower itself. You have a sympathetic victim, consigned at an early age to a downward spiral of working class living, through no fault of her own, a mother who treated her as a bouncing ball to be tossed back and forth between New England and The South if for no other reason than one less mouth to feed during economic upheaval. Short herself became one of the earliest 'throwaway kids', having to develop an armor of self-protection as she learned that home was impermanent, along with parental guidance. Like so many others before—and after—her, she found comfort from hard luck and despair in a bottle and seemed to rely upon the male comforts of enlisted men. I'm assuming they reflected an honor and stability she never found in her own father."

Dean continued, "The crime itself revives those unsettling elements which draw you in; moth to the flame type stuff: The Jack the Ripper style mutilations, the Lizzie Borden style reporting hysteria and one-upsmanship which complicated getting at any truth ultimately, and you can even toss in the Ted Bundy element of the defenseless young girl brutalized and killed. Without any solution, all of it is great fodder for speculation and the basis for as many stories as the mind can conceive springboarding from crime.

"Finally, you are left romanticizing how a young woman, dressed to the nines and being last seen in one of the classiest bars in Los Angeles' most elegant hotel, winds up chopped in half and dumped in a public park. It makes you want to spend some afternoons in the Millennium Biltmore Bar drinking and thinking of what course of events created The Black Dahlia."

While the Millennium Biltmore may have been more of a Hollywood "back lot" than any location in California, for that matter, any hotel in America aside from New York's Plaza Hotel, I am always somewhat amazed that scenes from two of my favorite noir films, *The Blue Dahlia* and *The Maltese Falcon*, weren't shot there. Of course, Dashiell Hammett's *The Maltese Falcon* starring Humphrey Bogart and Mary Astor, was set in San Francisco. And Raymond Chandler's *The Blue Dahlia* despite its stellar cast of Alan Ladd and Veronica Lake has been sternly criticized for its second-rate production values. Sets seem like they could have come from a low-budget Off-Broadway play. How much more ambiance would the Millennium Biltmore have lent the two great movies? Despite their somewhat hokey plots. But it should be remembered that *The Maltese Falcon* didn't just become a cult film years after it opened because Bogart, at least according to one authoritative poll, had become the number one male box office star of the last century. Even shortly after it opened no less than a "private" screening of the film noir was run for President Franklin Roosevelt and British Prime Minister Winston Churchill during a break in a White House Cabinet Meeting not long after the attack on Pearl Harbor.

Some of the most historic events at the Millennium Biltmore took place behind closed doors. Robert Caro, in his definitive book on President Lyndon Johnson, details the "staircase" diplomacy which went on at the Millennium Biltmore to pick John F. Kennedy's running mate.

"The drama that was to consume the rest of the day—Thursday, July 14, 1960—would play out on two sets in Los Angeles's Biltmore Hotel," writes Caro.

"One was on the hotel's ninth floor. It consisted of a large three room suite in one corner of the floor, together with a series of individual standard hotel bedrooms that stretched along a rather dimly lit corridor. All the interconnecting doors had been unlocked so that the suite and bedrooms comprised a single unit. During the hectic days earlier that week, this 'Kennedy suite' had become known by the number on the door of the big corner suite: 9333. The candidate himself slept every night in a hideaway apartment his father had rented for him, but during the day 9333 was his headquarters.

"The other set, two floors below and in the corresponding corner and corridor, also with a large suite and adjoining bedrooms stretching down the corridor, was 7333, the Johnson suite.(Johnson and Lady Bird slept there during the convention, as did their daughters.) John Connolly was in the first of the bedrooms, 7331, Walter Jenkins in 7330, and the rest of the staff had bedrooms further down the hall. Separating the two sets was the eighth floor, on which Robert Kennedy had a suite, 8315. Governor Lawrence had the big suite on the tenth floor, Stewart Symington on the sixth, Rayburn's suite was on the seventh floor with Johnson's, but at the opposite end of the corridor.

"The elevator in this section of the hotel was located near the far end of the line of bedrooms at the end of the corridor furthest from the corner suite. That morning what one reporter referred to as the 'pushy, sweaty mass' of the press-newspaper and magazine reporters and photographers, television cameras, cameramen and correspondence was clustered around the elevator's doors. Kennedy had arrived at his suite very early, before any reporters had arrived, and it was assumed he was still at his apartment and would come up in the elevator, and might emerge and provide them with a clue as to the identity of the vice presidential nominee.

"There was another connection between the two sets, however: a back staircase almost directly across from the 9333 door in the floor's corner—not a narrow back staircase, but a broad one, with a broad

RIGHT: JFK
BELOW: 1960
Democratic
Convention

open landing on each floor, as dimly lit as the corridors. If someone stepped out of the 9333 door of the Kennedy suite and walked almost straight across the hall and down the stairs, he had a good chance of avoiding the press, and that was what Jack Kennedy did, successfully, at about 10:15 that morning. Descending down the two flights of stairs, he knocked on the door of 7333."

The rest, as they say, is history. Until I started compiling this book I had not fully appreciated the importance of Los Angeles in the political careers of the Kennedys. JFK picked LBJ as his running mate at the Biltmore during the contentious 1960 Democratic Convention in the city, and eight years later, at another well-known L.A. hotel, the Ambassador, John's little brother Bobby was gunned down in the kitchen during his own run for the presidency that year.

It's just as I've always said. Hotels play an important part in the life of any community, and the greater the hotel usually the greater a part it plays. What if JFK and LBJ hadn't been staying at the Millennium Biltmore during the convention? What if they'd stayed at a hotel without such a convenient back staircase? Maybe John Connolly would have ended up Kennedy's running mate. Even worse, maybe the presidency that year would have gone instead to a certain California native—Richard Nixon. You see, it really does pay to stay at the better hotels.

The Democratic Convention in Los Angeles in 1960 was one of the last old-style conventions, where there was real drama as to who would be the party's selection, not only for President but Vice-President. Soon the new primary season system would be in place, giving the rank-and-file party members all over the country a much greater say in the outcome, but of course killing the great drama that often occurred at the convention itself. After the primary system started, the convention really became, as many have noted, just a three- or four-day television commercial.

I never got a chance to see what one of the old conventions was like first-hand, but during my heyday as a newspaper reporter I did during the 1984 Republican Convention in Dallas get the great opportunity to serve as Tom Brokaw's PR man. Brokaw, of course, the anchorman of NBC *Nightly News* for many, many years, was a bit of a throwback himself to the older style of politics. Dallas and Texas had only recently entered the ranks of the Republicans. During the 1960 Los Angeles Convention, of course, Texas, like the rest of the South, was a deeply Democratic stronghold. Ironically, it was Los Angeles at that time that was not squarely in the Democratic column. Arch conservative and Hollywood star Ronald Reagan in only a few years would be elected the Republican governor of California. So, times do change and politics certainly changes from era to era. The one thing that remains much the same is the swanky hotels the pols stay at during the festivities. A great hotel like the Millennium Biltmore can't afford to play politics, unless it wants to offend half its potential clientele.

11

Other Grand Los Angeles Hotels

Of course, L.A. has other historic hotels. Two of its most colorful, the Ambassador and Garden of Allah, are no more. The Beverly Hilton is a notable grand, but arguably doesn't have the history of the other two hotels. Known in recent years as where Whitney Houston died, but there were other happy occasions. One in1985 according to Nancy Nelson was "An Evening with Cary Grant". It was a 1000-dollar-a-plate black tie dinner, which attracted 940 of Cary Grant's most ardent admirers and friends. Nearly $1 million was raised to assist young talent in theater, dance, and film through scholarships.

The late American business icon E.L. Cord, who developed the Duesenberg for movie stars and other extremely wealthy individuals, originally leased the land for the Beverly Hilton Hotel. As a super salesman his personal mantra was not just to sell things but amaze potential buyers with the quality and uniqueness of his products such as the Duesenberg, sales of which plummeted during the Great Depression.

As with the Millennium Biltmore, the development of these other downtown Los Angeles hotels became a magnet for other types of urban expansion. Real estate executive Hank Elder, for instance, credits the building of the Beverly Hills Hotel with jump-starting the growth of Beverly Hills.

Located on a smallish parcel of ground, which once was the estate of screen star Alla Nazimova, the Garden of Allah, like the Bel Air or the Beverly Hills Hotels today, had a resort air, especially to New Yorkers who hailed from the canyons of Manhattan such as 44th Street where the Algonquin Hotel was once home to many stars like John Barrymore who preferred the Ambassador, and Dorothy Parker who liked the Garden of Allah.

When F. Scott Fitzgerald left Hollywood in 1927 he was already known as one of America's greatest novelists. *The Great Gatsby* had been published only two years earlier. Warner Baxter, who won the Oscar for Best Actor a few years later at the Millennium Biltmore, starred in the silent film version of the novel. (Unfortunately it has been lost. Perhaps, someday someone will discover a "vault" of classic old silents like this.) But when Fitzgerald returned to Hollywood ten years later, it was literally his last hurrah. He and his wife, Zelda, lived at the Ambassador the first time around. In the 1930s it was the Garden of Allah which had also seen better days. Still, it was grand, not in a physical sense like the Ambassador, or certainly the Millennium Biltmore, but its guests still were.

One of the pleasantest things about Los Angeles is that there are so many grand historic hotels which revolve as figurative spokes of a wheel around the "hub" of the Millennium Biltmore. There's a hotel for every taste and pocketbook. "The suite I was married in, the Rodeo Room, is still there. It's on the top floor, the big Crystal Room," said writer Jeffrey Davis. "I used to know the widow of the guy who owned the Beverly Wilshire. Hernando Courtright."

"I like the Beverly Hills. I have stayed at the Beverly Hilton, and the Beverly Wilshire which is a beautiful hotel, too," says Patty Farmer, the author of a fabulous hotel book, *The Persian Room Presents*, about the old nightclub in New York's Plaza Hotel. "The Beverly Wilshire is quite lovely. I've been to quite a few weddings there. I went to a wedding there going back maybe eight years and people ask what was the most spectacular wedding you've been to, and that was it!"

"She was an actress and she married a doctor and they were just over the top with party guests…it was the accoutrements and furnishings that were so outstanding. It was just a pleasure staying there for the weekend and it was lovely. I love the Polo Lounge at the Beverly Hills Hotel. And I've loved it consistently for more years than I'm going to admit to. It used to be 'the' place—the only place you'd take meetings ...and many, many people called the Polo Lounge their office. Movie deals were struck there."

"And deals for you?"

"Nothing I'm talking about!"

"Maybe not as much as in the older days, but the Polo Lounge is still significant. I was there with a business partner, Barbara, many times, and that's her unofficial office...and one time we were sitting there and Sandra Bullock was there...Dale Olsen just passed away. He was the legendary PR man. Too bad he's not around. He's told me Marilyn Monroe stories. And having lunch with him there—it was almost like holding court because everybody, young and old, came by the table. I don't think I've been there without seeing people I recognized and knew. Forget about people who are the writers and producers.

If the Millennium Biltmore became the backdrop of many movie and TV scenes, the Garden of Allah became a star. It became a play called *The Garden of Allah* and later a movie starring Marlene Dietrich and Charles Boyer. The movie had nothing to do with the famous hotel. In the movie Domini Enfilden, played by Dietrich, and a former trappist monk, played by Boyer, meet in the desert and fall in love. But the Hollywood intrigue associated with the name wasn't lost on many film fans.

To avoid reporters, George S. Kaufman left the Garden of Allah by stuffing himself in the back of a laundry truck. Kaufman's several exploits with star Mary Astor (*The Maltese Falcon* and many other classic films) had become headline news when a diary kept by Ms. Astor was quoted in the press.

"Errol Flynn always seemed to be staying at the Garden of Allah while in between marriages. In 1935 he married Lili Damita who had a villa at the Garden," wrote Hollywood historian Martin Turnbull. "He also shared a villa with actor David Niven and writer Bill Lipscomb in the mid-30s. He was there when Warners offered him *Captain Blood* (1935) which made him a star."

F. Scott Fitzgerald moved into the Garden of Allah in July of 1937. "Down on his luck and deeply in debt, MGM offered him a lucrative contract to write for the movies. His first important assignment there was *Three Comrades* which was ultimately rewritten by Joe Mankiewicz," Turnbull wrote. "Fitzgerald stayed at the Garden for about a year and then moved to a cottage in Malibu. While at MGM he worked on *Madame Curie* starring Greer Garson and *Gone With the Wind* but eventually only received one screen credit" (for *Three Comarades*).

The early 1930s, which spelled financial ruin for much of the country, was kinder to L.A. because its mainstay industry, the movies, was going great guns and the Millennium Biltmore, which had the added bonanza of hosting the Academy Awards for much of the decade, was no exception. The late actor, playwright and director Elliott Nugent, who cowrote the smash hit Broadway play *The Male Animal* with humorist James Thurber, says in his book *Events Leading Up to the Comedy*, that "Hollywood had not been hit so hard as the rest of the country.... The stock market crash and the Depression had dealt me a blow but not a killing one. Being out of a job was a new and terrible experience for many, but it has always been an ordinary situation for an actor."

Elliott Nugent also lived at the Garden of Allah during part of World War II. "We found we could not move into our own house in Bel-Air. The lessee had promised to get out on thirty days notice but the pledge was not in writing," Nugent says. "So we put up in a bungalow at the Garden of Allah. It turned out to be a rather interesting place; my father was living there as were Frank Sinatra, Kay Thompson [an actress and choreographer who went on to write the Eloise books about the little girl who lived at The Plaza Hotel], Louis Calhern...."

The Beverly Hills Hotel, also called the Beverly Hills Hotel and Bungalows, is on Sunset Boulevard. It "opened on May 12, 1912, before there was even a city called Beverly Hills," Wikipedia says. By 1914, actors and actresses such as Mary Pickford and Douglas Fairbanks, Charlie Chaplin, Gloria Swanson, Buster Keaton, Rudolph Valentino and Will Rogers soon built homes in Beverly Hills, transforming bean fields surrounding the Beverly Hills Hotel into prime real estate. L.A.

real estate executive Hank Elder's late grandfather sold lots in Beverly Hills for $4,000 each.

The original main building of the Beverly Hills Hotel was designed by Pasadena architect Elmer Grey, in a Mediterranean Revival style. Twenty-three bungalows are located in the gardens north of it. A new wing was added to the east side of the main building in the 1940s. The gardens of the grounds were designed by renowned landscape architect Wilbur David Cook. It was the first building in the greater area, leading to the creation of a surrounding city, and is often referred to by the local population and others as just The Hotel. Since the city's inception, the hotel has been a central meeting place for residents and business people, especially from Los Angeles's movie and television industries.

The popularity with royalty and celebrities continued to grow through the years. Guests included the Duke and Duchess of Windsor, John Wayne and Henry Fonda. Elizabeth Taylor's father had an art gallery in the lower level of the hotel. Howard Hughes lived at the hotel on and off for thirty years. The hotel was featured on the album cover art of the Eagles' 1976 LP *Hotel California*.

Svend Petersen, the Danish-American pool manager at the hotel for forty-two years, became a "Hotel Ambassador" in 2002. He had notably opened up the pool after hours for The Beatles and taught Faye Dunaway to swim a freestyle crawl for *Mommie Dearest*. He was also known for warning Southern California newcomers in no uncertain terms about the dangers of sitting out in the California sun too long.

On December 30, 1992, the hotel closed for a major restoration. It reopened on June 3, 1995, with many new room amenities. In 2012, the hotel celebrated its 100-year anniversary and began to remodel its lobby, with the Polo Lounge, pool cabanas and Cabana Café, and guestrooms and suites to be renovated by 2014. The hotel was also named the first historic landmark in Beverly Hills on September 12, 2012.

The original owners were Margaret J. Anderson and her son, Stanley S. Anderson, who had been managing the Hollywood Hotel. From 1928 to 1932, the hotel was owned by the Van Noy Railway News and Hotel Company. Its strict resident owner from 1954 until his death in 1979 was former Detroit real estate magnate Ben L. Silberstein, who took it over from Hernando Courtright, who became head of the Beverly Wilshire Hotel. Some of the hotel's owners have been celebrities: Irene Dunne, Loretta Young, and currently the Sultan of Brunei.

Marvin H. Davis bought the hotel for $54 million from Silberstein's sons-in-law Burt Slatkin and Ivan F. Boesky. Boesky had bought the five percent of stock that was outstanding and decided to sell, despite Slatkin's desire to keep the hotel. Less than a year later, Davis sold the hotel to Sultan Hassanal Bolkiah for $110 million. The hotel is managed and owned by the Dorchester Collection, organized in 1996 to manage the hotel interests of the Brunei Investment Agency. The west coast regional director for the Dorchester Collection oversees the Beverly Hills Hotel as well as Hotel Bel-Air.

"I've always tried to deal with people the way they are, what they like …Elizabeth Taylor—she was a delightful woman. She used to sunbathe near the pool. But once she got older, she got heavier so I offered her cabana #7, an upper cabana, and she sunbathed there," Svend said. "She was a delightful woman. Don't forget she helped so many people with AIDS and everything else. She was a great human being."

He continued in an interview poolside at the Beverly Hills, "the golden years of the 1960s and 1970s! But we still have golden years for the hotel. We improve so much every day. Now they are going to redo the pool….the 60s and 70s were not only the golden years for motion pictures but also the music business. I started at the hotel in 1959."

"Roddy McDowell was another great human being. He and Liz Taylor grew up together and became stars because there were a lot of stars who couldn't take it [being grown up stars]. Being a child star—it's difficult to grow up—look at Shirley Temple. She was sensational when she was little. She was cute as hell."

"I dearly loved Whitney Houston who came down here many times. She was here for three weeks one time. Every morning she came down and gave me a big hug and a kiss. Just so human and wonderful and you just hate to see her or anyone go to waste like that. Clive Davis, who is a good friend of mine, loves to stay here. He always had his special cabana 10. And she was in 11. And you feel so much for them. You almost feel like they are family...Mary Tyler Moore—she was just a delight. 'Good evening, Miss Moore,' I said. She said, 'What do you mean, Miss Moore? Mary! You're more famous than me!'"

The Beverly Hills Hotel was one of the first of the fine hotels built in Los Angeles. Beverly Hills was not even a city yet but its boosters wanted to be taken as seriously as any as a luxury hotel destination so in 1912 they opened the Beverly Hills Hotel.

The hotel enjoyed some success and helped put Beverly Hills, incorporated in 1914, on the map. Sadly the hotel fell to the lows many great buildings fell to during the Great Depression. In 1930 the hotel was overextended in its corporate and bank debt and shut its doors forcing the Bank of America (the mortgage holder) to step in.

Bank of America out of San Francisco wanted to get the hotel running as quickly as possible, using their people to manage it, otherwise it would start to get run down, and possibly convert it to residential as the bungalows were rented out. The bond holders on the other hand had debt issued by the corporate owner that was secured by the operating hotel which was the highest and best use as a hotel. Due to the various interests (there were numerous bond holders) it was a complicated situation brought on by the easy money during the roaring days of the 1920s.

The bond holders wanted to be bought out at a reasonable rate and the bank wanted to manage the hotel and pay them off later. In the end the bank needed to deal with the bond holders so the bank sent a vice president to Los Angeles as its representative and the bond holders elected a local businessman and fellow bond holder to represent their combined interest in the negotiations

Evidently the negotiations were very difficult and dragged on for some time. While these terms were being negotiated the bank's representative apparently dug further into the hotel and decided that he might like to be the manager. The man was named Hernando Courtright and he did go on to finalize the negotiations and to buy out the bond holders and ultimately put together the deal (as manager) to buy the hotel from the bank.

Courtright then went on to create the legendary Polo Lounge in the now famous (think "Hotel California" by the Eagles) Beverly Hills Hotel. Courtright did not stop there. After selling the hotel he made into a legend, in 1961 he went on to buy and expand the tired Beverly Wilshire Hotel at one of the most famous corners in the world—Rodeo Drive and Wilshire Boulevard.

Courtright wielded his magic at the Beverly Wilshire and the year before he passed away in 1986 sold the Beverly Wilshire for the huge sum of $125,000,000, after personally heading the hotel for over 25 years.

The tough business man in the Beverly Hills Hotel negotiations was none other than George W. Elkins who parlayed the money from those negotiations into a legendary real estate empire in Los Angeles. By coincidence or design, Elkin's corporate offices were two blocks south of the Beverly Hills Hotel and two blocks north of the Beverly Wilshire. Elkins died in 1993 at the age of 93, also still at the head of the empire he created.

Interestingly neither Hernando nor George ever did any business nor socialized together again after those fateful negotiations in the early 1930s.

Hernando Courtright "was" the Beverly Wilshire Hotel for many years. According to Christopher Matthew in his book, *A Different World*, the hotel is "a mixture of the grand and the intimate, the old and the new, the bizarre and the traditional, the European and American ..." Before his association with the grand hotels, Mr. Courtwright had been a banker with Bank of America in San Francisco. The bank found, in 1936, itself in possession of the Beverly Hills Hotel and with the financial help of film stars, including Jimmy Stewart, he bought the hotel and turned it into the heralded "Pink Palace," today part of the illustrious Dorchester Collection which includes the Dorchester in London and the New York Palace Hotel as well as the Plaza Athénée in Paris.

I was at the Bel Air in 1991, on a California book tour with my book on the Waldorf Astoria. I had lunch there with actress Natalia Nogulich, who had recently moved to L.A. from New York after starring on Broadway.

Some years later I was long-distance-dating a woman from L.A., and we stayed at the Bel Air. I soon—the next day—realized that in Hollywood SEX is not love, as is true the world over. But in a town that raised romance to a high art in classic films, I had fantasized the love was mutual. "I'm not in love with you and am seeing someone else," she told me as we were about to meet in Palm Beach.

The Bel Air Hotel is one of the most beautiful hotels in the world. Perfection of rooms, decorating, amenities set in a sea of floral and palm perfection.

The hotel has resumed a high part of a hotel experience. In the morning, before breakfast overlooking the Swan Pond, I fetched her fresh ice cream from the Bel Air kitchen. And she lay on her stomach, loving it. Our breakfast, as romantic and delicious as was humanly possible, also holds a special place in my hotel memories. And, yet, as I ascended the rather steep stairs to our second floor suite, I had a premonition of things shortly to come. I thought of Greta Garbo and screen star John Gilbert in a scene from *Queen Christina*, where Garbo, who had been Gilbert's real-life paramour, touches the walls of their rustic cabin and you know it is the last time she may see him.

Another grand hotel that has featured prominently in Oscar history then and now is the Roosevelt Hotel. The Hollywood Roosevelt Hotel, named after Theodore Roosevelt and financed by Douglas Fairbanks, Mary Pickford, Louis B. Mayer and other film luminaries, opened its doors on May 15, 1927. It hosted the presentation of the First Academy Awards in 1929 inside its Blossom Ballroom. Marilyn Monroe was a resident at the Hollywood Roosevelt for two years when her modeling career took off. Her first magazine shoot was taken on the diving board on the pool behind the hotel, which was recently removed. The hotel's remodeled pool contains an underwater mural painted by David Hockney. Today the hotel is a favorite of Oscar goers—and winners!

"After visiting the legendary Roosevelt Hotel, one couldn't help but feel nostalgic about old Hollywood and all it entailed," said Megan Saulsbury, CEO of Canyon PR. "Surrounded by luxury, history and elegance, the overall atmosphere of this renowned hotel is only celebrated further by the personal attention and service offered by each employee encountered. A truly classic experience."

The Ambassador Hotel hosted the Second Academy Awards on April 3, 1930, and five more times in that decade and the 1940s. Opening two years before the Millennium Biltmore, in 1921, the hotel hosted the Academy Awards the year *Gone With the Wind* won the Oscar for Best Movie in 1940. The Coconut Grove Nightclub first called the Coconut Grove was one of the hottest night spots in America where Frank Sinatra, Sammy Davis Jr., Judy Garland, Louis Armstrong and Diana Ross all performed. The hotel occupied nearly 24 acres at 3400 Wilshire Boulevard. Soviet leader Nikita Khrushchev stayed here when he visited America in 1959 and Marilyn Monroe did a photo shoot by the Ambassador pool.

In 1927, F. Scott Fitzgerald lived at the Ambassador before moving to Delaware. "As their last Hollywood gesture, they stacked all the furniture in the center of their Ambassador Hotel room and at the top of this impromptu altar they placed all their unpaid bills," Aaron Latham writes in his book *Crazy Sundays: F. Scott Fitzgerald in Hollywood*.

Presidents Roosevelt, Truman, Eisenhower, even Hoover, stayed here in its lush park-like setting. But when then U.S. Attorney General Robert F. Kennedy was shot in the pantry off the Embassy Ballroom in 1968 and died a day later, its fate was largely sealed.

"My father was a champion of those who suffered disadvantages in America. He was actively engaged in helping people help themselves through community action," said Maxwell Kennedy, son of Robert and Ethel Kennedy, on the opening of two pilot schools on the site of the old Ambassador Hotel. The schools appropriately called the Robert F. Kennedy Schools occupy the site of the historic old hotel where in 1968 Robert F. Kennedy was assassinated. That was eight years after Robert F. Kennedy and John F. Kennedy planned strategy for JFK's presidential bid in the Millennium Biltmore Hotel during the 1960 Democratic Convention.

"This new K-12 learning center will educate and empower our young people and their parents to fight for economic and social justice. I know of no better way to advance the living legacy of Robert Kennedy."

"The messages Robert F. Kennedy worked to deliver to us decades ago—that we can all be part of a change for a better world, a greater world—are alive with us as we celebrate the opening of not one, but two exciting new pilot schools here at Central Los Angeles Learning Center #1 K-5," Board President García said. "Years of commitment and struggle led by parents and the community come to fruition today as we mark profound change for students that now have two unique small schools dedicated to incorporating new and innovative methods of teaching."

The new elementary school site features two pilot schools (schools within the LAUSD—given charter-like autonomy over curriculum): University California Los Angeles (UCLA) Community School (UCS) and New Open World (NOW) Academy. Both schools provide students with an opportunity to continue their education on the same school site once the middle and high school portions of the larger campus are completed.

He's just Svend. That's what Katharine Hepburn, Dean Martin, Jerry Lewis and Warren Beatty know him as. And in many ways his charm, good looks, attention to detail as manager of the pool at the Beverly Hills Hotel is synonymous with the Beverly Hills, located on many lush acres in the heart of Beverly Hills.

Just beauty, charm, location, the Beverly Hills Hotel in Beverly Hills.

For actress Cindy Marinangel, a Chicago Second City Conservatory graduate and lifetime member of the Actors' Studio in New York, the Beverly Hills is her favorite.

"The Beverly Hills Hotel—there's nothing like it. You know what I mean," actress Cindy Marinangel told me. "That's where I go. Oscar day. If I'm dressed that's where I go for a drink…. It depends on what you're looking for. Depends on what you want? What are you looking for?"

Cindy is a Chicago Second City Conservatory graduate, having studied under Stephen Colbert and Nia Vardalos. She is a Lifetime Member of the esteemed Actor's Studio in N.Y. and L.A., currently learning from greats Martin Landau and Mark Rydell. In film, Cindy has starred opposite Fred Durst and Tim Bagley, and her latest feature, *LA Superheroes,* just won the Audience Award for "Best Feature" in the NY International Film Festival. Cindy can be heard narrating *E! Entertainment's* international special *Beyoncé Uncut* and has just appeared on German TV's Taff Channel in *Rockin' Los Angeles.* She is a member of SAG, AFTRA and AEA.

"The Chateau Marmont. That's very much my style," New York-based singer Steve Ross told me. "It's so exciting."

"I became more aware of it as I became an adult...Now it's the place where movie stars are. It's where Brad Pitt and Angelina Jolie and Lindsay Lohan and Leonardo DiCaprio go to the bar..."

The Chateau Marmont is also noted as where comedian John Belushi died in March 1982, in Bungalow 3 to be exact. Belushi had "partied" the previous night, and when his personal trainer, William Wallace, arrived at his bungalow, Belushi was already dead according to reports. Medics pronounced him dead at 12:45 and he was buried about a week later at Abel's Hill Cemetery in Martha's Vineyard. A memorial service was held at St. John Divine in New York the following day.

Bob Woodward covers Belushi's death at the Chateau in detail. But his book was roundly criticized by friends of Belushi's, including Dan Aykroyd.

In the beautiful book, *American Hotel Stories,* travel writer Francisca Matteoli singles out the Chateau Marmont for "all the stories that haunt and...for the ghosts and dreams that inhabit it, for its moments of madness and flamboyant extravagance."

"Montgomery Cliff convalesced here after the (auto) accident that nearly killed him," she writes in a chapter on the Chateau.

Jim Morrison, lead singer for The Doors, lived here during the 1970s. "He checked in to the Chateau Marmont the way people might go to stay with their grandmother," said one Hollywoodite.

Yet, she adds, his behavior was not the grandmotherly kind. "One night he attempted to get into his van by jumping through the window from the hotel roof.... The stunt cost him two broken ribs."

She waxes quite poetic in other prose. "The atmosphere [of the Chateau] is intimate, bohemian, part Gothic, part Spanish with the occasional dash of contemporary style."

"Light [in the lobby] filters in from the garden, and the view of trees and greenery, framed by the Gothic window gives the feeling of a medieval painting."

The hotel genius behind Chateau Marmont these days is André Balazs who also owns the trendy Mercer in New York and Standard in L.A. Balazs reminds me of another hotelier who I know better, Henry Kallan, who owns and manages the Elysee Hotel and others in New York and is building a major hotel in Toronto.

André Balazs is the President and CEO of André Balazs Properties, and he's as much a celebrity as some of the hotel's stars. His hotels include the Mercer Hotel in New York and Sunset Beach on Shelter Island. The Standard hotels include The Standard, Hollywood; The Standard, Downtown LA; The Standard Spa, Miami Beach; The Standard, New York; and the newest addition, The Standard, East Village, as well as the Chateau Marmont.

In his early years, Balazs worked at Biomatrix, a New Jersey-based bio-tech company founded by his father. In 1990 he purchased Chateau Marmont, subsequently launching his career as an hotelier.

Chateau Marmont is located at 8221 Sunset Boulevard. The building was initially built in 1927 as apartments. It was modeled loosely after the Château d'Amboise, an historic royal retreat in France's Loire Valley.

The hotel has 63 rooms, suites and bungalows that are set amidst private gardens where they offer panoramic views of the city.

In 1926 Fred Horowitz, a prominent Los Angeles attorney, chose the site at Marmont Lane and Sunset Boulevard to construct a premiere luxury apartment building. Horowitz had recently traveled to Europe for inspiration and returned to California with photos of a Gothic chateau along the Loire River. In 1927 Horowitz commissioned his brother-in-law, European-trained architect Arnold A. Weitzman to design the seven-story, L-shaped building based on his French photos. When deciding upon a name for the building, Chateau Sunset and Chateau

Hollywood were rejected in favor of Chateau Marmont, a name conceived from the small street running across the front of the property.

On February 1, 1929, Chateau Marmont opened its doors to the public as the newest residence of Hollywood. Local newspapers described the Chateau as "Los Angeles's newest, finest and most exclusive apartment house...superbly situated, close enough to active businesses to be accessible and far enough away to insure quiet and privacy." For the inaugural reception, over 300 people passed through the site including local press.

Check Out

The time has come again for me to pack my bags and depart these splendid accommodations and return to the far more plebian trappings of my New York apartment. Indeed, all good things must come to an end. But, as always whenever I stay at such a storied and historic and resplendent hotel as the Millennium Biltmore, I will take with me, along with the small bottles of shampoo, my fond memories, the remarkable tales I have heard, and overheard, and the new acquaintance of the charming people I have had the privilege of meeting and conversing with during my stay. From Chairman Kwek and Ms. Chan up in the executive suites down to the bellboys in the hallways and the busboys in the kitchen, it was a grand experience and a good education and, most importantly, a fun time.

It's true that I am a New Yorker at heart, but for a few glorious days, thanks to the Millennium Biltmore and its sterling staff, I was a traveler in a fantastic country, a guest of the stars and an imbiber of foods and spirits fit for the angels. Adios, amigos.

Appendix A

Movies, and Other Things, Shot at the Millennium Biltmore

In *Chinatown*, one of the best crime dramas since *The Maltese Falcon*, characters played by stars Jack Nicholson and Faye Dunaway meet at the Millennium Biltmore to discuss the murder of her husband. It's a wood-paneled restaurant with red leather banquets. Dunaway has a Tom Collins with a lime. When they step outside the restaurant, Nicholson as the private eye says, "When a wife tells me she's happy when her husband is cheating on her, it runs contrary to my experience." These are most certainly among the most placid moments in this film fraught with spine-tingling suspense. And this is just one of hundreds of movies shot at the Millennium Biltmore since 1923. A partial list of these films since 1975:

FEATURE FILMS

How to Make Love Like an Englishman	Southpaw Entertainment	October	2013
Chop Shop	AH Coyote Productions	October	2013
The Wedding Ringer	Screen Gems Productions	September	2013
Jersey Boys	Warner Bros. Pictures	September	2013
Imagined	Danny Collins Productions	August	2013
Baggage Claim	Sneak Preview Productions	November	2012
Delirium	World's Fair Pictures	October	2012
A Leading Man	ALM Productions	August	2012
Destiny the Stars and You	Attention Soldier Productions	December	2011
The Dark Knight Rises	Warner Bros. Pictures	October	2011
Valiant	RG Pictures	August	2011

Hotel Noir	Gato Negro Films	August	2011
J. Edgar Hoover	Warner Bros Pictures, Inc.	February	2011
Atlas Shrugged	"The Strike" Productions	July	2010
But Beautiful	One Zero Productions	July	2010
Like Crazy	Like Crazy LLC	June	2010
Bridesmaids	So Happy For You Productions LLC	June	2010
Beginners	Beginners Movie LLC	December	2009
Columbus Circle	G4 Productions	July	2009
State of Play	Universal Pictures	January	2009
State of Play	Universal Pictures	November	2008
Dam Love	Bollywood Hollywood Productions	August	2008
Dam Love	Bollywood Hollywood Productions	July	2008
Obsessed	Stage 6 Films, Inc.	May	2008
The Soloist	DreamWorks Productions, LLC	March	2008
National Treasure 2	NT2 Productions, Inc	May	2007
Iron Man	Iron Works Productions, LLC	May	2007
Rush Hour 3	Avery Pix, Inc	February	2007
Dreamgirls	DreamWorks, LLC	September	2006
The Great Buck Howard	20th Century Fox	September	2006
Spring Breakdown	Warner Bros Pictures, Inc.	August	2006
License to Wed	20th Century Fox	June	2006
The Little Man	Big Baby Productions, LLC	March	2006
Evan Almighty	Universal City Studio, LLLP	March	2006
In Justice	ABC, Inc.	January	2006
Commander-in-Chief	ABC, Inc.	January	2006
Flags of our Fathers	Warner Bros Pictures, Inc.	October	2005
42.4%	Gramercy Productions, LLC	April	2005
Grandma's Boy	Wilshire 1 Productions, LLC.	April	2005
Grandma's Boy	Wilshire 1 Productions, LLC.	March	2005
Syrianna	Warner Brothers, LLC	February	2005
7th Heaven	The WB TV Network	December	2005
Mission Impossible III	Paramount Pictures	December	2005
D-War	"D-War, LLC"	November	2004
Otherwise Engaged	Rose City Pictures, Inc.	August	2004
Rumor Has It	Rose City Pictures Inc.	August	2004
XXX 2	Revolution Films	July	2004
Cat Woman	Warner Brothers Pictures	June	2004
UntitledMartin Lawrence Project	20th Century Fox	June	2004
Miss Congeniality 2	Warner Brothers Pictures	May	2004
Beauty Shop	MGM Studios, Inc.	April	2004
Synergy	Universal Pictures	March	2004
Crash	Crash Productions, Inc.	March	2004
Wedding Crashers	Avery Pix, Inc.	March	2004

Appendix A

Shopgirl	Shopgirl, Inc.	December	2003
The Criminal	Warner Brothers Pictures	November	2003
Bride & Prejudice	Kintop, Inc.	November	2003
First Daughter	20th Century Fox	August	2003
First Daughter	20th Century Fox	July	2003
The Criminal	Warner Brothers Pictures	June	2003
Starsky & Hutch	Warner Brothers Pictures	June	2003
Paparazzi	Airborn Productions	April	2003
Cheaper by the Dozen	20th Century Fox	March	2003
Providence	Walt Disney Pictures	March	2003
Expert Witness	20th Century Fox	March	2003
Surviving Christmas	DreamWorks Productions LLC	December	2002
SWAT	Columbia Pictures	October	2002
House of Sand and Fog	DreamWorks Productions, LLC	October	2002
The Italian Job	Paramount Pictures	September	2002
Daredevil	20th Century Fox	June	2002
Bringing down the House	Disney Productions	June	2002
Austin Powers in Goldmember	New Line Cinema	December	2001
The Master of Disguise	Sony Pictures	November	2001
Stuart Little 2	Columbia Pictures	June	2001
Spiderman	Columbia Pictures	May	2001
The Sweetest Thing	Columbia Pictures	April	2001
Enough	Columbia Pictures	April	2001
Mr. Deeds	Columbia Pictures	April	2001
Ocean's Eleven	Universal Pictures	February	2001
Clockstoppers	Paramount Pictures	February	2001
The Cell	DNA Productions	December	2000
Dragonfly	MGM Universal Pictures	November	2000
Simone	Avery Pix, Inc.	October	2000
Project 95	TVM Productions, Inc.	July	2000
Heartbreakers	MGM Productions	May	2000
Rock Star!	Metal Productions	May/April	2000
Blow	New Line Cinema	April	2000
What Women Want	Paramount Pictures	March	2000
Thirteen Days	Warner Bros.	January	2000
Deuce Bigolo: Male Gigolo	Touchstone	Spring	1999
The Adventures of Rocky & Bullwinkle	Universal Pictures	April	1999
Blue Streak	Columbia Pictures	February	1999
Lost Souls	New Line Cinema	November	1998
The Debtors	BPL Films	October	1998
Fight Club	20th Century Fox	July	1998
Message in a Bottle	TIG/Warner Bros. Productions	July	1998

Title	Studio	Month	Year
8 MM	Columbia Pictures	April	1998
Cruel Intentions	Columbia Pictures	April	1998
Enemy of the State	Buena Vista Pictures	March	1998
Molly	MGM Productions	March	1998
Payback	Warner Bros.	October	1997
My Giant	Castle Rock Pictures, Inc.	August	1997
Primary Colors	Universal Pictures, Inc.	July	1997
The Game	Polygram	June	1997
Romy & Michele's High School Reunion	Touchstone Pictures	May	1996
My Fellow Americans	Warner Brothers	April	1996
Set It Off	New Line Cinema	January	1996
Grosse Pointe Blank	Buena Vista Pictures	January	1996
The Rock	Hollywood Production	January	1996
The Fan	Fan Production	January	1996
Escape From L.A.	Paramount Pictures	December	1995
Independence Day	Twentieth Century Fox	August	1995
The Nutty Professor	Universal Pictures	July	1995
In The Line of Fire	Castle Rock Pictures	May	1995
Forget Paris	Castle Rock Entertainment	November	1994
Speechless	MGM, Inc.	July	1994
Don Juan De Marco	Juno Pictures, Inc.	May	1994
Junior	Universal Pictures	May	1994
Little Big League	Castle Rock Prod., Inc.	February	1994
Beverly Hills Cop III	Paramount Pictures	October	1993
True Lies	20th Century Fox, Inc.	September	1992
In The Line of Fire	Castle Rock Pictures	December	1992
Dave	Warner Brothers	August	1992
The Distinguished Gentlemen	Buena Vista Pictures	June	1992
Hoffa	20th Century Fox, Inc.	April	1992
The Bodyguard	Warner Brothers	April	1992
Born Yesterday	Buena Vista Pictures	January	1992
Hero	Columbia Pictures, Inc.	January	1992
A Very Good Year	Castle Rock Production	December	1991
Final Analysis	Warner Brothers	October	1991
All I Want for Christmas	Paramount Pictures	July	1991
Stella	Samuel Goldwin	July	1991
Bugsy	MCA/TRISTAR	January	1991
Misery	Columbia	September	1990
The Five Heartbeats	20th Century Fox	April	1990
Another 48 Hours	Paramount Pictures	January	1990
Joe vs. the Volcano	Warner Brothers	June	1989
Ghostbusters 2	Columbia	March	1989

Appendix A

Fabulous Baker Boys	20th Century Fox	January	1989
Chances Are	Tri-Star Pictures	June	1988
Baby Boom	MGM	January	1987
Pretty in Pink	Paramount Pictures	July	1985
Beverly Hills Cowgirl Blues	CBS Entertainment, Inc.	May	1985
Firefox	Universal Pictures	January	1985
Hot Pursuit	NBC Productions	September	1984
Beverly Hills Cop	Paramount Pictures	July	1984
Brewster's Millions	Universal Pictures	May	1984
Ghostbusters	Columbia Pictures Features	February	1984
Young Doctors in Love	ABC Films	May	1982
Bachelor Party	20th Century Fox	October	1983
Masquerade	20" Century Fox	September	1983
The Adventures of Buckaroo Banzai	20th Century Fox	August	1983
Splash	Disney Productions	May	1983
Masquerade	20" Century Fox	March	1983
The Quest	Stephen Cannell Productions	September	1982
Dr. Detroit	Universal Pictures	August	1982
Star 80	The Ladd Company	August	1982
Pink Panther	Blake Edwards	February	1982
Rocky III	MGM	April	1981
National Lampoon Goes to the Movies	United Artists	January	1981
Posse	David Gerber Productions	January	1981
Foul Play	Paramount Pictures	December	1980
Continental Divide	Universal City Pictures	December	1980
Charlie Chan & the Curse of the Dragon	Queen American Citizen	June	1980
The Dollmaker	United Artists	April	1980
True Confessions	MGM	April	1980
A Change of Seasons	20th Century Fox	March	1980
The Group	Savage Beast Pictures	February	1980
Freebie and the Bean	Warner Brothers	February	1980
The Octagon	American Cinema Productions	January	1980
The Long Days of Summer	Dan Curtis Productions	October	1979
The French Atlantic Affair	M.G.M.	August	1979
Beggerman, Thief	Universal Pictures-NBC	August	1979
Altered States	Warner Brothers	May	1979
Bad News Bears	Paramount Pictures	May	1979
Baltimore Bullet	Film Fair	March	1979
Power	Columbia Pictures	February	1979
Blind Ambition	Time Life	January	1979

Airport '79	Universal Pictures	January	1979
The Foundation	Associated TV	October	1978
Ebony, Ivory, & Jane	Frankel Films	July	1978
Little Mo	Spelling Entertainment	July	1978
The Raid on Coffeyville	Dan Curtis Productions	May	1978
Evening in the Byzantium	Universal Pictures	May	1977
The Buddy Holly Story	Columbia Pictures	November	1977
Loose Change	Universal Pictures	May	1977
The Betsy	Harold Robbins International	September	1977
The Driver	20th Century Fox	August	1977
Blue Collar	TAT Communications	June	1977
The Other Side of the Mountain	Universal Pictures	June	1977
Faces	Faces International	March	1977
The Other Side of Midnight	20th Century Fox	December	1976
New York, New York	MGM	August	1976
King Kong	Paramount	July	1976
Billy Jack Goes to Washington	National Student Film Corp.	May	1976
A Star is Born	First Artists	March	1976
The Last Tycoon	Paramount	November	1975
Chinatown	Paramount	November	1974

WEEKLY EPISODIC TELEVISION

Glee	Twentieth Century Fox Television	April	2014
Mad Men Season 7	UROK Productions	April	2014
Scandal	ABC Studios, Inc.	March	2014
Revenge	ABC Studios, Inc.	March	2014
Revenge	ABC Studios, Inc.	February	2014
Castle Season 6	ABC Studios, Inc.	January	2014
HBO "Shameless"	Bonanza Productions Inc.	January	2014
Mad Men Season 7	UROK Productions	November	2013
Chasing Life	SPRODCO Inc.	November	2013
Revenge	ABC Studios, Inc.	October	2013
Heirs	Heirs, Inc.	September	2013
Chasing Life	SPRODCO Inc.	September	2013
Scandal	ABC Studios, Inc.	September	2013
Parks & Recreation	NBC Studios LLC	August	2013
Ironside	NBC Studios LLC	July	2013
Mad Men Season 6	UROK Productions	April	2013
The Newsroom	Farnsworth Entertainment	April	2013
NCIS: Los Angeles	CBS Television Studios	March	2013
Happy Endings	Remote Broadcasting	March	2013
Glee	Twentieth Century Fox Television	February	2013
NCIS: Los Angeles	CBS Television Studios	Februar	2013
90210	Eye Productions	February	2013

Appendix A

Mad Men Season 6	UROK Productions	January	2013
NBC Universal "Go On"	Open 4 Business Productions	December	2012
HBO "Shameless"	Bonanza Productions Inc.	October	2012
ABC Studios "Body of Proof" Season 3	FTP Productions	October	2012
NBC Universal "Go On"	Open 4 Business Productions	October	2012
It's Always Sunny in Philadelphia	Sunny Television Productions	October	2012
Scandal	ABC Studios	August	2012
NCIS: Los Angeles	CBS Television Studios	August	2012
Castle Season 5	ABC Studios	July	2012
Ringer	CBS Television Studios	January	2012
CBS Studios "The Mentalist"	Warner Bros. Television	January	2012
CBS Studios "The Mentalist"	Warner Bros. Television	December	2011
Mad Men Season 5	UROK Productions	December	2011
Touch	Twentieth Century Fox Television	December	2011
Ringer	CBS Television Studios	November	2011
Castle Season 4	ABC Studios	October	2011
Ringer	CBS Television Studios	October	2011
Perception	ABC Studios	Octobe	2011
CSI: NY — Season 8	CBS Television Studios	October	2011
House of Lies	Blind Decker Productions Inc.	September	2011
Castle Season 4	ABC Studios	August	2011
Prime Suspect	NBC Universal	August	2011
The Finder	Twentieth Century Fox Television	August	2011
Mad Men Season 5	UROK Productions	August	2011
Scandal	ABC Studios	August	2011
The League Season 2	New League Productions, Inc.	August	2011
House of Lies	Blind Decker Productions Inc.	July	2011
True Blood Season 4	Home Box Office	May	2011
NBC "The Event"	Open 4 Business Productions	February	2011
NBC "The Event"	Open 4 Business Productions	January	2011
CSI: NY — Season 7	CBS Television Studios	January	2011
TNT "Southland"	Warner Bros. Television	December	2010
HBO "Shameless"	Bonanza Productions Inc.	November	2010
Law & Order Los Angeles	NBC Universal	October	2010
The Cape	NBC Universal	October	2010
Curb Your Enthusiasm Season 8	Home Box Office	September	2010
CSI: NY — Season 7	CBS Television Studios	September	2010
House Season 7	NBC Universal	September	2010
Criminal Minds: Suspect Behavior	ABC Studios	August	2010
Desperate Housewives Season 7	ABC Studios	August	2010
Mad Men Season 4	U.R.O.K Productions, Inc.	August	2010
NBC Undercovers Season 1	Bonanza Productions	August	2010

TNT "RIZZOLI & ISLES"	Horizon Scripted Television	June	2010
Make It or Break It Season 2	PRODCO, Inc.	April	2010
Grey's Anatomy Season 6	ABC Studios	April	2010
CSI: NY — Season 6	CBS Television Studios	April	2010
24 Season 8	Twentieth Century Fox Television	March	2010
CSI: NY — Season 6	CBS Television Studios	February	2010
24 Season 8	Twentieth Century Fox Television	January	2010
Private Practice	ABC Studios	January	2010
The Forgotten	Bonanza Productions	December	2009
NUMB3RS	ABC Studios	December	2009
NCIS Season 7	CBS Television Studios	November	2009
LIE TO ME Season 2	Twentieth Century Fox Television	November	2009
CSI: NY — Season 6	CBS Television Studios	October	2009
Castle Season 2	ABC Studios	October	2009
24 Season 8	Twentieth Century Fox Television	October	2009
Chuck	Warner Bros. Television	September	2009
Castle	ABC Studios	August	2009
Mad Men	U.R.O.K Productions, Inc.	August	2009
Prom Queen	Michael Eisner's Vuguru	April	2009
Entourage	Home Box Office (HBO)	April	2009
Heroes	NBC Studios, Inc.	March	2009
Numb3rs	CBS Television Studios	January	2009
Dirty Sexy Money	ABC Studios	September	2008
Dollhouse	Twentieth Century Fox Television	August	2008
The Meant to Be's	CBS Television Studios	June	2008
CSI: NY — Season 5	CBS Television Studios	June	2008
24	Twentieth Century Fox Television	May	2008
ER	Warner Bros. Television Production	April	2008
Mad Men	UROK Productions	April	2008
CSI: NY — Season 5	CBS Television Studios	December	2007
The Shield	The Barn Productions	November	2007
Till Death	Montrose Productions	October	2007
Moonlight	Warner Bros Television Productions Inc	October	2007
Journeyman	20th Century Fox Television	August	2007
Dirty Sexy Money	ABC Studios, Inc	August	2007
Eli Stone	ABC Studios, Inc	August	2007
Nip/Tuck	Warner Bros. Television	August	2007
CSI: NY — Season 5	CBS Television Studios	July	2007
Mad Men	U.R.O.K Productions, Inc.	June	2007
Big Shots	Warner Bros Television Productions Inc	March	2007
Supreme Courtship	Twentieth Century Fox Television	March	2007
Without a Trace	Warner Bros. Studios	January	2007

Appendix A

CSI: NY — Season 4	CBS Television Studios	December	2006
Shark	CBS Television Studios	October	2006
Smith	Warner Brothers TV-LLC	October	2006
Daybreak	Touchstone Television, LLC	September	2006
CSI: NY — Season 4	CBS Television Studios	uly	2006
Damages	Twentieth Century Fox Television	March	2006
Capital Law	CBS Network Television/Paramount	March	2006
Heist	NBC Universal Studios, Inc.	March	2006
Vanished	Twentieth Century Fox Television	March	2006
Windfall	Twentieth Century Fox Television	February	2006
CSI: NY — Season 4	CBS Television Studios	January	2006
Commander in Chief	Touchstone Television Productions	January	2006
Injustice	Touchstone Television	December	2005
7th Heaven	Spelling Television	December	2005
Commander in Chief	Touchstone Television Productions	November	2005
Windfall	Twentieth Century Fox Television	November	2005
Boston Legal	David E. Kelly Productions	October	2005
The Last Time	The Last Time, LLC	September	2005
Alias	Touchstone Television Productions	September	2005
CSI: NY — Season 3	CBS Television Studios	September	2005
Commander in Chief	Touchstone Television Productions	August	2005
Crossing Jordan	NBC Studios	August	2005
Commander in Chief	Touchstone Television Productions	July	2005
Without a Trace	Warner Bros. Studios	July	2005
Diamond Weissman Project	20th Century Fox- Television	April	2005
The Catch	ABC-Disney Productions	March	2005
The Wedding Chapel	Granite Productions	March	2005
Eyes	Warner Bros.	February	2005
NYPD-Blue	Bochco Media, LLC, Inc.	February	2005
NYPD-Blue	Bochco Media, LLC, Inc.	January	2005
Blind Justice	Bochco Media, LLC	January	2005
CSI: NY — Season 3	CBS Productions	January	2005
Without a Trace	Warner Bros. Studios	November	2004
Stamo's Project	20th Century Fox Television	November	2004
Hells Kitchen	Upper Ground Enterprises, Inc.	October	2004
Alias	Touchstone Television Productions	October	2004
CSI-Las Vegas	CBS Productions	October	2004
Cold Case	Warner Brothers Television	September	2004
West Wing	Warner Brothers Television	September	2004
Girlfriends	Paramount Productions	August	2004
Cold Case	Warner Brothers Television	August	2004
Boston Legal	David E. Kelly Productions	July	2004
Adventures in Love	All Hands on Deck	April	2004
Drew Carey Show	Warner Brothers Television	April	2004

Joan of Arcadia	Canterbury Productions	April	2004
Alias	Touchstone Television Productions	February	2004
Cold Case	Warner Brothers Television	February	2004
Judging Amy	20th Century Fox	January	2004
Cold Case	Warner Brothers Television	January	2004
Miss Match	20th Century Fox	December	2003
The Handler	Viacom Productions	December	2003
Judging Amy	20th Century Fox	October	2003
Without a Trace	Warner Brother Television	September	2003
Skin	Warner Brothers Television	August	2003
Crossing Jordon	NBC Studios,Inc.	March	2003
Boomtown	NBC Studios, Inc.	February	2003
The Guardian	Rosecrans Production	December	2002
Without a Trace	Warner Brothers Television	December	2002
Mr. Sterling	Raleigh Studios	October	2002
The District	CBS Productions	October	2002
West Wing	Warner Brothers	October	2002
Crossing Jordan	NBC Studios	September	2002
Angel	20th Century Fox Televison	August	2002
West Wing	Warner Brothers	August	2002
Couples	Touchstone Television	April	2002
The Court	Warner Brothers	March	2002
Leap of Faith	Universal	February	2002
The Division	Viacom Production	February	2002
The Agency	CBS Productions	January	2002
Leap of Faith	NBC Studios	January	2002
Little John	McGee Street Productions	January	2002
West Wing	Warner Brothers	December	2001
Felicity	Touchstone Television	November	2001
The Agency	CBS Productions	October	2001
The Agency	CBS Productions	October	2001
Thieves	Warner Brothers	October	2001
Citizen Baines	Warner Brothers	September	2001
Citizen Baines	Warner Brothers	September	2001
The Agency	CBS Productions	September	2001
West Wing	Warner Brothers	August	2001
Alias	Touchstone	August	2001
Leap of Faith	NBCS Productions Inc.	April	2001
The Court	Touchstone Television	April	2001
Once and Again	Once and Again Productions	March	2001
Providence	NBC Productions	March	2001
The Tick	Sony Television	January	2001
The West Wing	Warner Bros. Television	December	2000
Bull	TNT	December	2000

Appendix A

Ally McBeal	20th Century Fox Television	October	2000
Providence	NBC	October	2000
Family Law	Arlington Productions	October	2000
Freakylinks	20th Century Fox Television	September	2000
The West Wing	Warner Bros. TV/NBC	April	2000
The West Wing	Warner Bros. TV/NBC	March	2000
Judging Amy	20th Century Fox Television	April	2000
Felicity	Warner Bros. TV/WB	February	2000
That 70's Show	FOX Broadcasting	January	2000
Providence	NBC Productions	December	1999
Time of Your Life	FOX Broadcasting	November	1999
Party of Five	Columbia Pictures TV/FBC	November	1999
The West Wing	NBC/Warner Bros. TV	August	1999
The West Wing	NBC/Warner Bros. TV	July	1999
Columbo	Universal Pictures	February	1997
JAG	Paramount	January	1997
NYPD Blue	FBC/Steven Bocho Productions	November	1996
Murder One	20th Century Fox / NBC	August	1996
ER	Warner Brothers / NBC	October	1995
AlienNation	20th Century Fox / FBC	May	1995
Chicago Hope	20th Century Fox / CBS	August	1994
Beverly Hills 90210	Fox TV/ Spelling Entertainment	October	1993
Lois & Clark	Warner Brothers / ABC	January	1994
Lois & Clark	Lorimar Productions	April	1993
Sisters	Lorimar Productions	August	1992
Civil Wars	Steve Bocho Productions	March	1992
Civil Wars	Steve Bocho Productions	January	1992
Civil Wars	Steve Bocho Productions	April	1991
Reasonable Doubts	Lorimar Productions	December	1991
Reasonable Doubts	Lorimar Productions	November	1991
Adventures of Mark & Brian	What's On First Prod.	August	1991
Murder, She Wrote	Universal Pictures	November	1993
Murder, She Wrote	Universal Pictures/CBS	July	1993
Murder, She Wrote	Universal Pictures/CBS	November	1991
Murder, She Wrote	Universal Pictures/CBS	October	1991
Murder, She Wrote	Universal Pictures/CBS	August	1991
Murder, She Wrote	Universal Pictures/CBS	August	1989
Murder, She Wrote	Universal Pictures/CBS	April	1988
Murder, She Wrote	Universal Pictures/CBS	January	1988
Murder, She Wrote	Universal Pictures/CBS	July	1987
Murder, She Wrote	Universal Pictures/CBS	October	1986
Murder, She Wrote	Universal Pictures/CBS	October	1984
The Trials of Rosie O'Neil	The Rosenzweig Co.	January	1991
Gabriel's Fire	Lorimar Television	November	1990

ThirtySomething	ABC	May	1989
L.A. Law	20th Century Fox /NBC	March	1989
The Law & Harry McGraw	Universal Pictures	March	1987
Falcon Crest	Lorimar / CBS	May	1987
The Colby's	Aaron Spelling / ABC	March	1987
Scarecrow & Mrs. King	Warner Brothers / CBS	January	1987
Matlock	Viacom Prod.	December	1986
The Colby's	Aaron Spelling Productions	October	1986
Cagney & Lacey	Orion Television	August	1986
Cagney & Lacey	Orion Television	October	1984
Cagney & Lacey	Orion/ Filmways Productions	March	1983
Cagney & Lacey	Orion Television	December	1982
Hill Street Blues	M.T.M. Enterprises /NBC	July	1986
Hill Street Blues	M.T.M. Productions	March	1984
Finder of Lost Loves	Aaron Spelling Productions	March	1985
Moonlighting	ABC Circle Films	March	1985
Crazy Like a Fox	Columbia Pictures	March	1985
Paper Dolls	United Artists	August	1984
Glitter	Aaron Spelling Productions	March	1984
Matt Houston	Aaron Spelling Productions	December	1983
Hart to Hart	Columbia Pictures T.V./ABC	September	1983
Mike Hammer	Columbia Pictures T.V./ABC	September	1983
Falcon Crest	Lorimar Productions/ABC	November	1983
Falcon Crest	Lorimar Productions/ABC	June	1983
Bare Essence	Warner Brothers/CBS	April	1983
Bare Essence	Warner Brothers/CBS	March	1983
Bare Essence	Warner Brothers/CBS	February	1983
Bare Essence	Warner Brothers/CBS	January	1983
Remington Steele	M.T.M. Enterprises/NBC	March	1983
Modesty Blaise	Paramount Pictures	April	1982
Paper Dolls	ABC	March	1982
The Phoenix	Australian Broadcasting Co.	March	1982
Bare Essence	Warner Brothers/CBS	June	1982
Dynasty	Aaron Spelling Productions	October	1981
Knot's Landing	Lorimar Productions	February	1981
Lou Grant	M.T.M. Enterprises	November	1980
Charlie's Angels	Spelling-Goldberg	March	1980
Hart to Hart	Spelling-Goldberg	August	1979
SuperTrain	Dan Curtis Productions	January	1979
The Bionic Woman	Universal Pictures	February	1978
Kojak	Universal Pictures	October	1977
Kojak	Universal Pictures	June	1977
Kojak	Universal Pictures	December	1974
Kojak	Universal Pictures	August	1974

Appendix A

Kojak	Universal Pictures	June	1974
Wonder Woman	Warner Brothers	July	1977
Family	Spelling-Goldberg	January	1977
Switch	Universal Pictures	August	1976
Switch	Universal Pictures	November	1975
Baretta	Universal Pictures	September	1975
Columbo	Universal Pictures	August	1975
McMillan & Wife	Universal Pictures	August	1975

TELEVISION MINI-SERIES

The 70s	NBC Productions	January	2000
Family Album (Danielle Steele)	NBC Productions	August	1994
The Winds of War	Paramount Pictures	November	1981
Scruples	Warner Brothers	August	1979
Roots	Warner Brothers	November	1978
Rich Man, Poor Man	Universal Pictures	May	1975

TELEVISION PILOTS

Guilt by Association	Turner North Center Productions	March	2014
The Brink	Muffin Magic Productions	January	2014
You're the Worst	Worst Productions	November	2013
Boomerang	WB Studio Enterprises	March	2013
Cinnamon Girl	Pacific 2.1	November	2012
Save Me	Remote Broadcasting	March	2012
The Asset	20th Century Fox Television	March	2012
Scruples	Warner Bros. Television	March	2012
Living Loaded	FX Network	March	2012
Free Agents	NBC Dark Toy and Big Talk Productions	September	2011
Revenge	ABC Studios, Inc.	September	2011
Special Investigation Los Angeles	20th Century Fox Television	April	2011
Friends With Benefits	20th Century Fox Television	April	2010
In Security	Turner North Center Productions, Inc.	March	2010
Chaos	20th Century Fox Television	March	2010
Undercovers	Bonanza Productions	February	2010
Rex Is Not My Lawyer	Open 4 Business Productions	December	2009
Supreme Courtships	20th Century Fox Television	March	2007
Capitol Law	NBC Productions	March	2006
The "DA"	Warner Brothers	February	2004
The Flannery's	Warner Brother Television	March	2003
The Lion's Den	Twentieth Century Fox	March	2003
Mr. Sterling	NBC Productions	March	2002
Life's Too Short	20th Century Fox Television	May	2000
Homicide	Lorimar Television	October	1991

Hotel | Aaron Spelling Productions | April | 1983

CABLE/PAY-PER-VIEW

NBA All Star	NBA Entertainment	February	2011
52nd Annual GRAMMY Awards	The Recording Academy	February	2011
Latin Fury 14 Press Conference: Antonio Margarito	Top Rank	April	2010
Fight Announcement: Julio Cesar Chavez, Jr. vs. Luciano Cuello	Top Rank	March	2009
Fight Announcement: Shane Mosley vs. Mayorga	Golden Boy Promotions	September	2008
Fight Announcement: Roy Jones Jr. vs. Joe Calzage	Square Ring, Inc.	September	2008
Fight Announcement: Casamayor vs. Marquez	Golden Boy Promotions	July	2008
Fight Announcement: Oscar de la Hoya vs. Steve Forbes	Golden Boy Promotions	May	2008
Fight Announcement: Nikolai Valuev	Don King Productions	September	2006
Windfall	NBC Productions	February	2006
Monk	NBC Productions	June	2006
Six Feet Under	Six Feet Under Productions	January	2005
Dinner for Five	Big Frog Productions	September	2004
Monk	O.P.P.I. Productions	May	2004
The Assistant	Super Delicious	April	2004
Six Feet Under	Six Feet Under Productions	March	2004
Medical Mystery	Paramount Television	March	2004
Curb Your Enthusiasm	Curb Your Enthusiasm, Inc.	July	2003
Path To War (HBO)	Guns and Butter Productions	October	2001
Running Mates	Turner Network Television	February	2000
Running Mates	Turner Network Television	January	2000
Fight Announcement: Trinidad-Reid	Don King Productions	January	2000
Fight Announcement: Holyfield-Lewis	Don King Productions	October	1999
Gia (HBO)	GIA Productions	July	1997
Weapons of Mass Destruction	HBO Productions	June	1997
Stranger Things (ShowTime)	Castle Rock Entertainment	June	1994
Heidi Chronicles	Showtime	November	1994
Tyson	HBO Productions	September	1994
And The Band Played On	HBO Productions	December	1993

MOVIE-OF-THE-WEEK/ T.V. SPECIALS/REALITY SHOWS

America's Got Talent | Marathon Productions | February | 2014

Appendix A

Germany's Next Topmodel Season 9	Redseven Entertainment GmbH	December	2013
Match	MyTeeVee.com	August	2013
The X Factor	Blue Orbit Productions	August	2012
Ultimate Dance Mom	Fly Girls Productions	July	2012
Liz And Dick	Silver Screen Alta Productions	June	2012
MTV 2 Yo!	MTV Raps MTV 2	January	2012
Betty White's Birthday Special	NBC Studios	January	2012
BET Master of the Mix Season 2	Wonderful 8 Productions	December	2011
High School Musicals	OWN Network	December	2011
Hell's Kitchen Season 9	Upper Ground Enterprises	May	2011
The Millionaire Matchmaker Season 5	Green Bottle Pictures	April	2011
The T.O. Show Season Two	VH1: Dissident, LLC	April	2011
Germany's Next Top Model Season 6	Tresor TV Produktions	March	2011
Poker Stars Season 1	Redseven Entertainment	February	2011
The Next Food Network Star	CBS Eye Productions	February	2011
The Real Housewives of Beverly Hills	Evolution Media	January	2011
Face Off	SyFy Network: Gemini 3 Prods.	October	2010
America's Got Talent	Marathon Productions	October	2010
Germany's Next Topmodel Season 5	Tresor TV Produktions	February	2010
America's Next Top Model Season 13	Anisa Productions	April	2009
Mission Hollywood	Tresor TV Produktions	March	2009
Germany's Next Top Model Season 4	Tresor TV Produktions	January	2009
Germany's Next Top Model Season 3	Tresor TV Produktions	March	2008
On The Lot	Mark Burnett Productions	April	2007
Germany's Next Top Model Season 2	Tresor TV Produktions	March	2007
Clean House	Style Network	November	2006
American Idol Season 6	American Idol Productions	September	2006
National Treasure	Declaration Productions	February	2004
Bad Boys 10	Bad Boys Entertainment	February	2004
Boston Public	Kelly Productions	August	2001
An American Tragedy	TVM Productions	July	2000
Stranger Things	Castle Rock Productions	June	1994
Mother's Boys — The Allison Gertz Story	12700 Productions Inc.	February	1992
Sinatra	Warner Brother	April	1992

Columbo - ABC Mystery Movie	Universal Pictures	August	1991
Some Kind of Love	Pipeline Production	August	1991
Babe Ruth	Lakeside Productions Inc.	June	1991
Columbo - ABC Mystery Movie	Universal Pictures	September	1989
Fatal Vision	NBC Productions	June	1984
Lottery	Orion Television Productions	December	1983
Jacqueline Bouvier	ABC Circle Films	June	1981
Dial 911	Papazian Productions	March	1981
The Man in the Santa Claus Suit	Dick Clark Productions	October	1979
Bob Newhart Comedy Hour	Greg Harrison Productions	December	1979
Dean Martin Show	Greg Harrision Productions	October	1976

ADVERTISEMENTS/COMMERCIALS

Audi	RESET	February	2014
Maybelline	Redseven Entertainment GmbH	January	2014
Milk	Tool of North America	January	2014
Call of Duty	MJZ Productions	January	2014
Kia	MJZ Productions	December	2013
AAA	Arts & Sciences	December	2013
Sega	Station Film	September	2013
Cadillac Doors	White Label	August	2013
Nike	Imperial Woodpecker	July	2013
Infinity	Gorgeous, Inc.	March	2013
Bold	M3 Studios	March	2013
Buick	Tool of North America	February	2013
Toyota	Believe Media	January	2013
Barclays	Logan Media	December	2012
ING	Direct Epoch Films	December	2012
Priceline	Skunk	December	2012
Esurance	MJZ Productions	October	2012
Revlon	Saville Productions	May	2012
Christian Dior "Miss Dior"	Stardust Visions	March	2012
Syfy The Stranded Promo	Leroy and Clarkson	March	2012
Hewlett Packard	The Sweet Shop	February	2012
Powerball	Skunk LLC	January	2012
Carbonite	Anonymous Content	January	2012
Directv	MJZ Productions	January	2012
Las Vegas	Hungryman	August	2011
Chevy Cruze	Duroo Productions	April	2011
Samsonite	Kelly Co	March	2011
Acura	Liquid Air Entertainment	March	2011
Rockport	exposureUSA	March	2011
California Lottery	Über Content	January	2011
Groupon	Go Films	January	2011

Appendix A

AT&T Wild Soccer USA "Landon Donovan"	Biscuit Films	December	2010
	Wild Soccer USA	September	2010
Chico's Brands Commercial	Bauerfeind Productions	June	2010
Mercedes Benz	Ink & Oranges	May	2010
General Motors Commercial	Aero Films	May	2010
Emporio Armani Underwear Campaign	Serial Pictures	April	2010
Full Tilt Poker Commercial	Moxie Pictures	February	2010
Audi — The Boston Episodes	Acne	December	2009
First Wave	LRN Productions	September	2009
Volvo	Caspar & Co. Productions	September	2009
Chivas Regal Ad Campaign	Legend, Inc.	August	2009
Monster.com	Epoch Films	December	2008
Zales	MJZ Productions	August	2008
General Mills	Mr. Big Film, Inc.	April	2008
Ford Focus	Bandito Brothers, Inc.	February	2008
Diet Pepsi	White Label-Product, Inc.	January	2008
A-1 Steak Sauce	Smuggler, Inc	November	2007
AT & T	Smuggler, Inc	September	2007
State Farm Insurance	Believe Media, Inc	August	2007
NFL-TV-Promo	Moving Parts, Inc.	June	2007
Folgers	HSI, Inc.	May	2007
Mc Donald's	Anonymous Content	January	2007
Full Tilt Poker	Moxie Pictures Inc	January	2007
Hyundai	JDH Productions, Inc	December	2006
Chevrolet	Pictures in a Row	December	2006
Master Card	Hungry Man, Inc.	May	2006
Jaguar	Pictures in a Row	April	2006
Farmers Insurance	A Band Apart	April	2006
Barclay's Bank	MJZ Productions	January	2006
IBM	Pytka Productions, Inc.	November	2005
Propel Water	Epoch Films	November	2005
Nissan	Backyard Productions, Inc.	October	2005
Clairol	Harvest Films	August	2005
Clairol	Harvest Films	August	2005
UPS	Anonymous Content	August	2005
LX/GX Lexus	Cente Productions	June	2005
Sony	Bravo Zulu, Inc	March	2005
Chrysler Commercial	Pictures in a Row	February	2005
Singulair	HKM Productions, Inc.	February	2005
T-Mobile	Epoch Films, Inc.	February	2005
Kelloggs-"Cinnamon Toast Crunch"	Green Dot Films, Inc.	February	2005

Heineken	Anonymous Content, Inc.	December	2004
Microsoft	RSA, Inc.	October	2004
William Lawson-Scotch	Atomik Pictures, Inc.	September	2004
Dunkin Donuts	MJZ Productions	September	2004
Toyota Camry	MJZ Productions	August	2004
Citroen	Plum Productions	July	2004
Robinson May	Plum Productions	July	2004
Holiday Inn-Express	Moxie Films	May	2004
Lexis	MJZ Productions	April	2004
Sprint	Harvest Inc.	April	2004
Honda	Tuesday Films	March	2004
Cadillac	Partizan	February	2004
Oil of Olay	Believe Media	January	2004
Lux	Seville Productions	December	2003
Microsoft	Light Room, Inc.	October	2003
Chrysler	Dektor Film	July	2003
Yahoo.com	Smuggler Productions	May	2003
Lux	Seville Productions	March	2003
Toyota	Downtown Reel	April	2003
Plavix	Radical Media	March	2003
Lux	Seville Productions	January	2003
Cisco	Radical Media	December	2002
Tylenol	Crossroads Films	December	2002
Visa	Moxie Pictures	September	2002
Toyota	Go Film Inc.	September	2002
Nissan	Radical Media	June	2002
Motorola	Radical Media	January	2002
Taco Bell	Anonymous Content	December	2001
Land Rover	Plum Productions	October	2001
Honda	Tuesday Films	June	2001
Revlon	Maxie Picture	March	2001
Siebel	HKM	January	2001
Conoco	Coppo Films	January	2001
Fredericks of Hollywood		June	2000
Sprite	Wind Mill Lane Productions	April	2000
Careers.com		April	2000
Honda	Bianglala Picture	February	2000
Motorola	Unknown	January	2000
Hotjobs.com (Super Bowl XXXIV)	McCann-Erikson Advertising	December	1999
Redken	Cornerstone Pictures, Inc.	November	1999
Merrill Lynch	Epoch Film	November	1999
Lexus	Dame Production Co.	September	1999
Lexus	Werts Films	November	1991

Appendix A

Maybelline	Dextor Higgins	March	1994
Maybelline	Dextor Higgins	January	1993
Sony	Hi Vision M Company	September	1996
Rolls Royce	Splash Productions	December	1996
Unocal 76	Johns and Gorman Films	November	1995
Ghurka Baggage	The Image Factory	January	1994
Wilson Leather	Red Dog Productions	July	1993
SAAB	Palomar	September	1993
U.S. Spirit	Harmony Pictures	March	1992
Skytel	Luna Pier Films	May	1992
MCI	Melody Films	July	1992
IBM	Perterman Moss, Inc.	July	1992
Gillette	Kira/H. Productions	April	1992
Burger King	Michael/ Daniels	May	1992
American Express	B.F.C.S.	December	1992
Smoking Patch	Highlight	November	1991
Delta Airlines	Petermann Films	October	1991
Canon Printers	Werts Films	August	1991
Citibank VISA	Weiland Films	June	1991
Virginia Slims	The Power & Lights Co.	May	1991
Sprite	Don Guy & Associates	September	1989
Dollar Rent-A-Car	AC&RJCCL Adv., Inc.	March	1989
Pan Am Airlines	unknown	April	1988
Schlitz Beer	Propaganda	March	1987
Pierre Cardin	Petermann Dektor	October	1986
Seagram's	River Run Films	February	1985
Kinney Shoe	Fred Levinson Productions	January	1984
Dr.Pepper	Film Fair	August	1983
Quaker Oats	Denny Harris	April	1982
Datsun	Kramer/ Racklen	July	1981
VISA	Flint Productions	July	1981
Datsun	Creative Enterprises	September	1980
Martel Cognac	Jerry Sims Productions	August	1980
Ford	Cooper, Dennis & Hirsch, Inc.	September	1979
Coca-Cola	Denny Harris, Inc.	July	1979
Oltas	Creative Enterprises	June	1979
Diners Club	Cooper, Dennis & Hirsch, Inc.	December	1978
Sony	Sun West Productions	December	1978
May Company	Pasetta Productions	June	1978
Magic Mountain	N. Lee lacy Productions	April	1978

MUSIC VIDEOS / VIDEOS

Alexander Kogan	Noisy Boy Music	May	2011
Tank	Riveting Entertainment	July	2010

Daughtry	Streetgang Films Inc.	October	2009
Anjulie "Rain"	Harvest Films	August	2009
Lostprophets	Rockhard Films	July	2009
Daniel Powter	DNA Inc.	September	2005
Wall Flowers	Smuggler Films	April	2005
Simple Plan	FM Rocks	December	2004
Yoga Video	American Video Group	November	2001
Son of a Gun — Janet Jackson	DNA, Inc.	November	2001
Son of a Gun — Janet Jackson	DNA, Inc	September	2001
Overprotected — Britney Spears	DNA, Inc	September	2001

INTERVIEWS / PHOTO SHOOTS

America's Book of Secrets	Prometheus Entertainment	January	2014
Gansevoort Las Vegas	Cherry On Top Inc.	May	2013
The Expendables 2	Rolling Thunder Productions	August	2012
History Channel Ancient Aliens	Prometheus Entertainment	March	2012
History Channel Ancient Aliens	Prometheus Entertainment	February	2012
History Channel Ancient Aliens	Prometheus Entertainment	January	2012
Teen Vogue	Peter McClafferty, Inc.	December	2011
Dateline NBC	NBC News	November	2011
Hidden City	Crazy Legs Productions	August	2011
HD Net "Dan Rather Reports"	HD Net	June	2011
Buddy Miller featuring The Majestic Silver Strings	New West Records	March	2011
Meg Whitman for Governor 2010	Meg Whitman for Governor 2010	October	2010
NBC Universal "Undercovers"	NBC Universal	February	2010
The Black Dahlia-Press Junket	Universal Studios	September	2006
Blue Alert-Photo Shoot	Horse Pictures, Inc.	December	2005
Peek and Cloppenberg	World Locations, Inc.	November	2005
Samsung-Still Shoot	Diane Mc Arter Productions	July	2005
Mercury Interactive-Photo Shoot	QAS Productions, Inc	July	2005
Miller-Still Shoot	Bill Charles, Inc	April	2005
Wataniya	Lightroom Inc,	March	2005
Corbis-Still Shoot	Corbis Corporation, Inc	March	2005
IBM	North Six, Inc,	February	2005
Mr Romance	The Oxygen Network	December	2004
Cocktails with Tony	The Walz/O'Malley Company	July	2004
People Magazine	People Magazine	June	2004
Dana Ba'el	High Tech Fashions, Inc	June	2004
Dirt Off Your Shoulders	Radical Media	February	2004
Game with a Fame	PMK/HBH	February	2004
Rancid	Sonet Film, AB	January	2004

Appendix B

My Father's Exclusive Interviews with Some Hollywood Heavyweights

My father, Ward Morehouse (he never used the "Jr." or "II"), was quite a well-known New York columnist in the middle of the last century. But like many a celebrity or social columnist in those days, much of his material depended on folks visiting from the Left Coast. Dad spent some time dallying with penning Hollywood scripts himself, and in tasting the Los Angeles waters, but his true métier was newspaper writing.

Here he is opining about that most famous Broadway and Hollywood acting couple of all, the Lunts.

Alfred Lunt was interviewed by my father around the time Lunt & Fontanne appeared in *The Visit* at the Biltmore Theatre. I am quoting his interview in its entirety as it goes a long way toward explaining their and others' celebrity during the so-called Golden Age of Broadway, which, depending on who you talk to, ended around the time they appeared in *The Visit* in Los Angeles.

I offer this snippet from a family time capsule because I think it captures quite well not only the "style" of newspaper columns of that bygone Golden Age, but also the aura surrounding such grand institutions as the Millennium Biltmore during its earliest heyday:

Consider Alfred Lunt. He is an American actor and he has acquired the renown of such institutions as U. S. 66, Mount Rushmore Memorial, Schlitz beer, the Ford Motor car and Kill Devil Hill, from which the brothers Wright soared in a flying machine just sixty years ago.

Alfred now says: "Lynn and I have no plans. We've got to find something that we're crazy about, that we're really simply mad to do. There's no great hurry. It's very pleasant here in Wisconsin and we'll just stay until something happens."... All of these were his words, as spoken to me via long distance from the village of Genesee Depot.

Alfred is from Waukesha, Wisconsin. He and his wife and his costar, Lynn Fontanne, now occupy their Swedish manor house, Ten Chimneys, near the tracks of the Rock Island Railroad and about fifteen miles from Waukesha. Their marriage has been tremendously successful for 40 years. That also goes for their careers, which are intermingled.

They've risen to the top of their profession in this country of ours and have been acclaimed across the world. Just the other evening, the television screen, via the presentation of Barrie's "The Old Lady Shows Her Medals," served to remind millions that the Lunts are sheer theater. They brought the real theater to the living rooms and bedrooms of the nation, certainly to mine. The resonance of Alfred's voice captivated his listeners, as did the electricity and flexibility of Miss Fontanne.

Alfred is America's First Actor and nobody has come close to him for 40 years. His artistry excels that of John Barrymore and of all the others, Holbrook Blinn included, who have been along since Jack played the Prince of Denmark. He's at the top of the list, certainly my list, and just as Lynn Fontanne had been the outstanding actress of her time. Only Laurette Taylor, who created Amanda Wingfield in "The Glass Menagerie," as many theater devotees know, is thought of as highly.

But this is Alfred's story. I'll give you later an appreciation of the remarkable Miss Fontanne.

All of this is being written to emphasize the point that the American stage needs Lunt & Fontanne. If employed regularly in the Broadway area they could give magnificence to a sagging theater. London's West End sends us Laurence Olivier and John Gielgud, Ralph Richardson and Paul Scofield, but not one of them is in Alfred's class. Our stage shrieks for his presence, and on a permanent basis. It took an old play like "The Old Lady Shows Her Medals," televised to jolt young and old alike into the realization that there's nothing wrong with the stage, or the Broadway phase of it, that Lunt & Fontanne can't cure.

Alfred's life has been one of devotion to the theater. He came up the hard way, playing trifling roles with the Castle Square Stock Company in Boston. He was in Cleves Kinkead's "Common Clay," and he appeared as an exuberant undergraduate in "Strong Heart," as a Balkan soldier in "Graustark," as a red, red Indian in "The Girl of the Golden West." Booth Tarkington, man of letters, and a magnificent gentleman, wrote a comedy, "The Country Cousin," and he was so impressed by Alfred's performance that he went backstage and told the stunned young actor that the next Tarkington play would be for him. That play turned out to be "Clarence." Alfred came to New York with it and he was on his way.

His performances since "Clarence" were in competition with other extraordinary performances of the times—John Barrymore in "Richard III," Richard B. Harrison in "The Green Pastures," Holbrook Blinn in "The Play's the Thing," Walter Huston in "Dodsworth," Louis John Bartels in "The Show Off." Characterizations in "Reunion in Vienna" and "Idiot's Delight" came later.

I wish that television could provide a weekly program for Lunt & Fontanne. I also wish that they'd think seriously of giving up Genesee Depot for two or three years for a triumphant return to Broadway, even though they had to revive such dated relics as "The Great Divide" and "The Witching Hour."

Anyway, here's to Alfred and Lynn, and may God bless them.

And here's my columnist father waxing wise on none other than that great man of letters, W. Somerset (*Of Human Bondage*) Maugham. As with the Lunts, you may not think of Maugham as "Hollywood" but you'd be wrong. Sure he was English and lived most of his remarkable life on the Côte d'Azure, but he made as much of an impression on the Hollywood of his era as any writer living. He was even portrayed on film at least once in the movie version of his great novel *The Razor's Edge*, starring Tyrone Power. (The fairly substantial part of Maugham went to that great British star Herbert Marshall.)

Novelist and playwright W. Somerset Maugham at an early age became one of the most famous writers in the world. One of his most famous novels, *Of Human Bondage*, became a movie with Bette Davis. He attended war bond parties at the Millennium Biltmore. How instrumental Maugham was in getting Jeanne Eagels to star in the 1929 film version of his novel *The Letter* I don't know. What I do know, based on my father's interview with the master writer, was that he was utterly surprised by the Broadway success of the play *Rain* which was based on his own short story.

In 1965 my father wrote of Mr. Maugham:

A grizzled face I know well, a face I've seen in the South of France, in the Far East and in the islands of the Pacific, in New York and in London and along the Champs Élysée in Paris, came upon the television screen in my bedroom tonight—and how welcome it was: I'm writing of the distinguished playwright, novelist, short-story writer, essayist and about-the-world traveler, W. Somerset Maugham.

I did my first interview with Mr. Maugham at Nelson Doubleday's beautiful home at Oyster Bay, L.I. He was then in his eighties, but he was articulate and outspoken and we got along as two friends who had first met in Pago Pago.

He said: "I made up my mind thirty years ago to retire from the theater. After all, success is something for young men. He said that "The Circle" was probably his favorite of all of his plays and he realized that he would have to accept the Public's Judgment on his novel, "Of Human Bondage."

"I wrote 'Of Human Bondage' in 1915. Nelson Doubleday told me some years later that they were still selling 20,000 copies a year. I have never seen 'The Circle' on any stage...I was astounded by the success of 'Rain' in New York. I absolutely couldn't believe it. Poor Jeanne Eagels. What a magnificent actress! I saw the part of Sadie Thompson played in many countries and in many languages but no one ever touched her. ...I can honestly say that from all my plays the performance that gave me the greatest satisfaction was that of Ethel Barrymore. She had great skill and a wonderful command over her audiences."

As the movies drew more and more Broadway stars west, one columnist in the *Los Angeles Times* even went so far as to claim the Rialto, which originally was comprised of blocks bordering the Herald and Times Square theater districts, had relocated to Los Angeles:

"It would pay the city of Los Angeles a fat revenue if it imposed a duty upon all New Yorkers who come out here to locate, especially if it made the tax retroactive. It could collect on half the population of Hollywood. Personally, I would be tickled to death to pay the tax if I had an opportunity.

"I glared about me at the Hollywood Arena one night when a couple of young exponents of the Manly Art of Scrambling Ears were smacking each other about in the ring, and I saw enough ex-big-towners around the ring to make a human chain from the Battery to Spuyten Duyvil. That is, if they were placed end to end, of course.

"I saw Mr. Lou Anger, now manager of Buster Keaton, who was once a hoofer and comedian of parts 'way back yonder' in the days when he teamed with Henry Dixon in vaudeville. I heard Henry just before I left New York. He was at the corner of Forty-eighth street and I was six blocks away, but that is only whispering distance for Henry. They say Mr. Lou Anger is rich. Henry isn't.

"But Mr. Lou Anger is a fine gentleman, and he knows the movie racket backward and forward. Some don't know it even one way.

"I saw Mr. Buster Collier, whose dad, Willie, is dean of the Friars' Club. It

Appendix B 167

seems but yesterday that Buster was about knee high to a grasshopper around New York. I saw Lefty Flynn, who made a reputation playing in Yale's backfield some thirteen years back, and I remember signing Lefty up to write articles on football for our publication when he was a sort of Red Grange of his time in reputation.

"Everybody along the Rialto in Los Angeles seems to be doing well. That pleases me immensely. Any time everybody else is doing well there is always a chance for the rest of us."

This columnist added:

"...I am pleased to report that it has been located. The Rialto of America has been re-established in Los Angeles, California...."

"...In New York I would never see an actor or theatrical celebrity of any kind at large, except on the stage, or in a club. Nowadays they live out on Long Island, or hide away in cavernous apartment houses far uptown, and it is difficult to find them without a search warrant."

"In Los Angeles they are all over the place. You can stagger from actor to actor in the lobby of the Millennium Biltmore at almost any time of the day or night. If you miss an actor, you will collide with a playwright or song writer, or perhaps a stage director, or producer, such as Mr. Dave Bennett. There should be Los Angeles chapters of both the Friars and the Lambs."

My father was not the only New York theatre person to head west, you know, as you will see in the following interview with Louise Dresser, a star who strutted the boards with the great George M. Cohan and other luminaries of the World War I period.

"Ms. Dresser is not to be confused with the now better known Hollywood actress Marie Dressler. Ms. Dressler, who died back in 1934, attended several Oscar nights at the Millennium Biltmore. Perhaps Dressler's most famous film exchange came in with blond bombshell, Jean Harlow in 'Dinner at Eight.' 'Do you know, machinery is going to take the place of every profession?' Harlow told Dressler in the film. 'My dear,' Dressler retorted, 'that is something you need never worry about.'"

In one of my father's Broadway After Dark columns, he wrote, "It was Christmas night in the year of 1914. There was a big opening at the Casino, a musical play, 'Lady Luxury,' being brought in with a cast including the frolicksome [sic] Ina Claire. But there was an even bigger opening at the Astor Theatre: George M. Cohan's revue, 'Hello Broadway,' had its premiere performance. Louise Dresser, with her singing of Cohan's 'Down by the Erie Canal,' was the show-stopper in that one.

"Now, in accordance with my where-are-they-now activity, I've just located, with an assist from Hedda Hopper, the long-absent-from-Broadway Miss Dresser. She's living in Glendale, Calif. And is quite as spirited as she was in her Broadway days.

"'I'm now a nice old lady of eighty four and a half,' said Miss Dresser when I reached her by telephone at her Glendale house. 'I'm happy and I love my friends, old and new. I've been inactive lately but I do hope to get just one more look at Broadway. I'm told that the Astor is still just where it always was. I did love that theater.'

"'Hello Broadway' was another Cohan & Harris hit. They were showmen who had the success touch. Cohan was in the original cast and so were William Collier, Charles Dow Clark, Petty Wood, Rozaika Dolly (of the Dolly Sisters), Lawrence Wheat and Florence Moore. Miss Dresser, now in retirement, has fond memories of the jaunty Cohan and his able and imaginative partner, Sam H. Harris.

"Christmas-time of 1914 was also brightened by the arrival of James Ferber's winning comedy, 'The Show Shop' Patricia Collinge, actress and writer, now living in Manhattan, had an important role."

My father interviewed another Hollywood actor much later, Carroll Nye, who was featured in *Gone with the Wind*. Nye, who became a Hollywood publicist, was married to Helen Lynch, a "WAMPUS Baby," one of a group of women in Hollywood who it was thought might become a big star.

"Carroll Nye is now a Hollywood publicist, engaged in the glorification of a profession he no longer calls his own," my father wrote.

Nye played Frank Kennedy, Rhett Butler's immediate predecessor, in *Gone with the Wind*. Scarlett was scornful of Kennedy—he reminded her of a timid brown field rabbit—but he had a store in Atlanta, as well as cash, and she was determined to save Tara from the tax collector. Within two weeks after she decided to marry him, she was Mrs. Kennedy.

"I don't usually talk about my acting career," said Nye the other day, "but 'Gone With the Wind' was a historical event and I am glad to have been a part of it." He started out as a juvenile in motion pictures and one of his early leading ladies was Loretta Young.

"I'm a Westerner and I had to pick up a Georgia cracker accent for 'GWTW,'" he said. "Will Price, a Georgia football star who later married Maureen O'Hara, was my speech coach. All of us wanted to go to Atlanta for the premiere, but the studio took only a few of us. It was a big disappointment."

"I hadn't seen Vivien Leigh since we made the picture until she came here in 'Duel of Angels' two or three years ago. My wife and I went backstage to see her, and my wife was so awed she couldn't say a word. Vivien is still beautiful, and a great lady."

Other Hollywood figures who came to the Millennium Biltmore were, according to one Broadway After Dark column:

Scott Miller (Duke Shannon of "Wagon Train")—"I'd never done any acting until I went in to the movies, and it shows. Now I'm very happy with what I'm doing, and I hope 'Wagon Train' goes on for 14 years. I'll stay with it as long as they have a job for me."

Billie Burke—"John Drew was the favorite leading man of my life, so gentle and so kind. People used to say he just stood there and didn't act, but of course he was acting all the time…Flo (Florenz Ziegfeld, her late husband) had a wonderful taste in everything. He insisted on good meals and we had them. A woman should run the house for the man."

Sam Jaffe, of Broadway and television—"The technicians are the wizards of movies and TV. There's nothing they can't do, no problem they can't solve… My last Broadway play was 'The Lark,' with Julie Harris. She's a charming person and very gifted. Her 'Victoria Regina' on television was an excellent portrait."

Chuck Connors, who will play a defense attorney in the new television series "Arrest and Trial"—"To be a good lawyer all you have to do is have a good researcher, have a good memory, and be an extrovert. All the great lawyers had the star touch; the court was a stage to them. A good trial lawyer is a better actor than an actor. This series is the best thing that ever happened to Ben Gazzara (his co-star). It gives him a big stage."

Appendix C

My Stepmother, the Bon Vivant

It's only fair that I give my famous stepmother equal time here with my famous father. Jean Dalrymple, my father's second wife and perhaps the most well known of his four wives, set me up in her living room on West 55th where I wrote my Broadway column for the *New York Post*. My father first met Jean when she was working for Broadway producer John Golden as his receptionist and "generally making myself useful," she said.

"*Strange Interlude* was still playing at his theater and it never failed to thrill me to be able to walk out through Mr. Golden's 'secret door' onto the balcony and watch various scenes which were my favorites," she once wrote.

When all was quiet in the office—everyone left early as Mr. Golden liked to get to Bayside for a nap before dinner, and the moment he took off, the place was deserted except for me—I dimly could hear the wonderful voices of Lynn Fontanne, Tom Powers, Earl Larrimore and my favorite, Glenn Anders (I had fallen in love with him in *They Knew What they Wanted*). I could not hear the words, but by the intensity of the sound I knew about where they were in the play and out I would pop through the little door and in the magic of the theatre, feeling a very specially privileged person.

Mr. Golden could not keep newspapermen from coming to see me. Ward Morehouse was one of the first. My impression of him was that he looked like a very attractive owl. He was short and comfortably plumpish, but far from fat. He had a wonderful fresh, fair skin, dazzling white teeth, lovely wavy brown hair and huge round blue eyes behind extra large tortoise shell glasses. He was soft spoken in a southern way and had a touch of wit and imagination in everything he said. I liked him immediately.

He often told me afterward how he came in and found "this grave little girl" who very efficiently gave him all the information he needed. He then asked if he could see "the great man" for a minute or two, and I was very pleased when Golden came to the door and personally ushered Ward into his office with all his charm and heartiness. I had been worried for fear Golden would object to this newspaperman visiting me, but of course, Golden thought that Ward had come only to see him.

When Ward left, Golden called me into the office. "What's going on here?" he asked.

"I don't know. What's going on?"

"Why, for God's sake," Golden suddenly roared, "Ward didn't come here to interview me! What do you think he wanted?"

"I don't know!"

"You don't, eh? Then I'll tell you! He walked in here and said, 'John, I'm going to marry that press agent of yours and I want you to be the first to know it!'"

I laughed. "I'll have something to say about that!"

"Well," Golden said, "make sure you say the right thing. Don't let me catch you marrying one of those newspaper bums."

About an hour later a special messenger from Cartier's appeared at the office. He handed me an interesting looking little white package. In it was a beautiful wrist watch and a card saying: 'This is only the beginning. I shall have something for you every day. W.M.'

I took it in and showed it to Mr. Golden, thinking it rather funny, but very nice. I said I thought I should return it.

"No, don't do that," Mr. Golden advised. "We can't afford to hurt his feelings. Not right now—just before an opening! I guess you'll have to play along with him until we get *That's Gratitude* on. But watch out for him! He's from Georgia and those southern boys have a way with them."

Ward did have a way with him, and in spite of Golden's warnings, I saw a great deal of him. I simply could not resist going to opening nights with him. Not only because he was wonderful company, but because through him I met virtually all of the important newspapermen and critics. Ward was very popular with them and, as he told me later, he enjoyed showing off his "little girl from Morristown" who, he said, was a welcome change from his usual string of eager ingénues.

When *That's Gratitude* did open, it received unanimously favorable notices and was a smash hit. Again my name was never mentioned in connection with it, but I did get royalties from it. Both John Golden and Frank Craven had reputations of being slightly penurious, but as far as I was concerned, I found them extremely generous. Golden, of course, went on to become a philanthropist in later years. Frank Craven was not only generous with money but also with praise, and to the end of his life he was a source of great comfort to me.

Ward used to have a section of his column called "The Passing Show," in which he listed the names of celebrities at each opening. He always included my name. O.O. McIntyre, Bide Dudley, Sidney Skolsky, Louis Sobol and F.P.A. also mentioned me from time to time, usually as having been at an opening with Ward.

One day John Golden called me into his office. It was the morning O.O. McIntyre had written in his column, "My wife, Mabel, says John Golden's press agent, Jean Dalrymple, has the loveliest complexion of any of the regular first-nighters."

Golden had O.O.'s column in front of him. "So now you're a regular first-nighter!" he said.

I had seen the item and knew it would nettle him. "Yes," I admitted, "I'm very fortunate. When I don't go with Ward, one of the other boys takes me, and really, since you don't let me go to the newspaper offices, I get a lot of work done with them all during the intermissions."

"Well," Golden said a bit grudgingly, "I must say you get a lot of space. I have to congratulate you on that Grantland Rice golfing column on Frank Craven. It's the first time a show of mine got onto the sports page. Did you meet Grannie at an opening night?"

"No, I met him at a cocktail party Ward took me to. I reminded him that Frank Craven is a good Golfer and did a golfing play for you, *The Nineteenth Hole*, and so he made a story of it for us."

"Oh, hell," Golden said, "I guess that's the new way of doing business. I myself never go to cocktail parties or opening nights." I thought to myself, well, you're an old man now and it's too late to change. (He was fifty-four!)

Since Ward was not a critic then and his "Broadway After Dark column in the *New York Sun* had been written and filed before we went to the theatre (except for "The Passing Show," which he had his assistant, good old Willie Priori, phone in for him, unless he took care of it himself), we often went after the openings to the company parties or to Tony's on West Fifty-second Street. Tony's was the habitual hangout of the drama department newspapermen and the young advertising executives as well as theatre folk.

Hollywood beckoned after *New York's Town*, a play my father and Jean Dalrymple wrote, was bought for a movie.

"Ward wanted Mayor Walker to perform the ceremony at City Hall," Dalrymple said. "When they learned we were to be married, Keats Speed, managing editor of the *New York Sun*, and his wife, Fawkie, who were good friends of Ward's and mine, insisted that we be married in their apartment by their minister, Dr. Ralph Sockman of the Park Avenue Methodist Church...."

Vinton Freedley [a major Broadway producer of his day and my godfather] was best man, and since my father was off travelling somewhere, Mr. Speed [editor of the *New York Sun*] gave me away.... All my old friends were there... Bert Lahr, Lillian Boardman and others from my vaudeville days were there, too. But there was no Mr. Golden. Ward and I left for California the next day on the Twentieth Century.

We got off at Pasadena, which was the chic thing to do, and Miriam Hopkins, with car and chauffeur, was there to meet us. Miriam, also from Georgia, had been Ward's close friend all the time he had been working at Warner's (and for years before in New York), but she was being very gallant about the marriage. She not only came personally but also had been kind enough to make all arrangements for our social life before our arrival. Also, she had rented a beach house for us to "honeymoon" in—Carmel Myer's beautiful little cottage at Santa Monica.

When we reached the beach house gloom settled on me. It was just dusk. The electricity had not been turned on, and we felt rather than saw our way around. Miriam chatted to me gaily all the time, pointing out the unseen beauties of the place and its many disadvantages, such as no linens, no blankets, no silver, no dishes or cooking utensils and water, electricity and gas still to be turned on. Also, there would be servants to find and such minor gems as a gardener and a "watchman" for the young bride to locate.

But thank goodness, Ward had kept his bungalow at the Garden of Allah, and there eventually we went to leave our bags and to change into dinner clothes for my first Hollywood party—the Richard Rodgers' wedding anniversary do.

The moment I walked into bungalow 8, happiness returned. Mrs. Ross, the woman manager of the Garden, had filled the little apartment with flowers, many of which had been sent by welcoming friends, and also she had strewn rice about in every room in circles around the flowers and she had put little mounds of it on all flat surfaces, including the bed. The place and atmosphere enchanted me, as well as the names on the cards that had come with the flowers. "Jimmy Cagney," said one card; "Cary (Archie Leach) Grant," said another; ... and "Fred Astaire," said an especially jolly one.

In the wonderfully equipped little kitchen, Miriam and I made coffee for all of us. Ward wanted to write a "Hollywood After Dark" column about the Rodgers party, and he went to work the moment we arrived. Of course, everyone who was anyone was there. I met Ward's producer, Darryl Zanuck, and his beautiful wife, Virginia, for the first time and also our director, Mervyn LeRoy, who was escorting Ginger Rogers. Within the first half hour after our arrival, we had ten or twelve invitations for dinner and just as many for cocktail parties. One of the invitations came from—I almost went into a Victorian swoon when I was introduced to him!—John Gilbert. I could not believe it when he singled me out and actually steered me to a corner of the room where we could sit and talk about—of all things—golf. Jimmy Cagney had told him I was a golfer and it seemed that this had become a veritable passion with John. We made a date to go out and play the very next morning and when Ward finally came to gather me up to go home, he found me still gabbing with John, flanked by Jimmy Cagney on one side and Cary Grant on the other.

He seemed almost annoyed by this and, bowing, said "Queen, if it suits your majesty, the chariot awaits." We all though this very funny; even I did—then. When we finally were back in our bungalow—not late, as Hollywood parties broke up early in those days, and still do—we piled into our nice big double bed.

No matter how late we went to sleep, Ward always has at work on his column for the *New York Sun* by six-thirty or seven, before taking off for the studio. He is a hunt-and-peck typist, very fast and very noisy, and he would bang furiously away while I made breakfast for him, the only meal I ever had a chance to prepare in our beautiful little kitchen. We had decided to live at the Garden of Allah, but since the beach house was already paid for, we had weekends at Santa Monica. It was a delightfully luxurious arrangement. In fact, everything was delightfully luxurious.

Miriam Hopkins finished a film and took off for New York and Europe, leaving us her two servants, Tell, her chauffeur-butler and Mary, his wife, a marvelous cook. Like Ward and Miriam, they were from Georgia, and magnificent-looking, with their flashing white teeth lighting up their handsome coal-black faces in ever-ready winning smiles. I loved them, and they were wonderful to me, both of them babying me and "making over" me, as Ward put it, in a way which took me back to the days with the Murphy family and Miss High in Morristown. They soon had the Santa Monica house slicked up and open, and we decided to give a housewarming on Sunday.

Usually one sits around the first half hour or so of a party and begins to feel like Charlie Chaplin in *The Gold Rush*, but for our first 'big' party the guests began arriving before noon, and for the next twelve hours, everyone who was anyone piled in there for swimming, games and lots and lots of eating and drinking. Recently I found a shopping list I had made out for that party. It started: "Forty frying chickens, ten pounds of black eyed peas... Prohibition was supposed to be in force, but I never saw any sign of it, ever, as long as I was with Ward. I still did not like more than a sip or two of wine. If only I had taken up serious drinking in those days, my life with Ward would have been an easier one. I guess I really was a little on the prissy side, and Ward was half right when he would roar at me, "You're a damned Sunday-School teacher, that's what you are!"

Soon Ward said that he could not possibly sleep in the same bed with anyone, and forthwith our nice double bed was exchanged for twin beds. Then a few weeks after that we left our darling little cottage for a large rambling one on the other side of the pool, with two bedrooms, one for each of us. Natalie Schafer, who visited us from New York, remarked acidly, "That's a quick disintegration of a love match, even for Hollywood."

Ward said I was, and always would be, "a little girl from Morristown," and he absolutely could not stand my "insane desire" to cook for him. Once, however, he did give in and let me fuss over a special dinner, for just the two of us. I had spent the whole afternoon preparing the things I knew he liked the best. He picked at them for a while in forlorn silence and then suddenly he burst into tears.

I was terrified. "What on earth is the matter?" I cried.

"I can't bear it," he sobbed. "That's all! I just can't bear it! We're in the most glamorous town in the world where we could be out having a glamorous time, and instead here we sit alone like a goddamned couple from the Bronx!"

There still was no word at all from John Golden who had not so much as sent me a telegram for my wedding. But then came a letter from Dixie French. He wanted to know if and when I would be coming back to New York and what my plans were because Mr. Golden was producing a new play by Rachel Crothers and Rachel insisted upon having me do the publicity. I at once happily replied that it wouldn't be long before we'd be back at the Essex House and that I'd like nothing better than to have my old job back. Ward was not at all pleased by this, however. He said he wouldn't stand for Golden having me "under his thumb" again, but I told him we'd manage that part of it when we got to it.

When the time came, we decided to fly back to New York. Flying was an adventure in those days, nicely informal, too, and casual. There were only a few daring passengers on our plane, and the pilot went off the course several times to take us sight-seeing—over the Grand Canyon for one thing—and once he swooped down and chased a herd of antelope for Ward's benefit. We flew (one hundred twenty miles an hour) only by daylight since there were no beacons or beams, and spent the night in Kansas City, finishing up the trip the following day. Apartment 3802 at the Essex House, when we reached there, was filled with flowers and, of course, people, but I went directly to the John Golden Office.

Appendix C

Rachel Crother's new play, *When Ladies Meet*, would be produced in New York in the fall and was to be tried out in Dennis, Cape Cod, that summer. I asked anxiously for Mr. Golden and Dixie said, "He's still sore at you, but he's getting over it. He'll call you himself one of these days, you'll see and say, 'Come home, all is forgiven.'"

And that is the way it was. One day Golden called me and we had a long luncheon. All was forgiven, but I never went back to him completely. Ward would not permit it. I could be John Golden's press representative, he declared, "but not his office slave!" I spent a few hours each morning with Golden, however, because I really loved working with him, and then there was the tryout of *When Ladies Meet* to be prepared and other interesting projects.

My father stayed at the Garden of Allah almost exclusively when he was in Hollywood to write movies.

Hollywood beckoned after *New York's Town*, a play my father and Jean Dalrymple wrote, was bought for a movie. It was at this time that Jean and my father decided to marry and then head west to adapt their script to film. The marriage and their west coast honeymoon were as bustling and animated as Manhattan rush hour traffic. It didn't take long for Jean to begin to see to the inklings of the kind of married life my father expected, as opposed to the kind of married life she envisioned.

New York City soon beckoned and my father and Jean had to return to their "normal" lives in The Big Apple. The change of scenery did nothing toward any concessions regarding how to live within a day-to-day marriage: but Job One for my step-mother was to resolve the silence of her "boss" John Golden.

Quoting from Jean's *September Child:*

When I returned to apartment 3802 from my office in the evenings, there was always a party going on. I never knew whom to expect, but it was almost always someone fascinating. Dorothy Parker, for instance, might be there, exchanging "cracks" with Ward. Those were the days of the so-called "amusing insult," originated by Alexander Woollcott, I guess, and definitely carried on by Ward, who fancied himself as sort of Woollcott's understudy. I never appreciated this form of "wit."

In those days Ward was very amusing and well organized. He usually got up about seven o'clock, went down to his office and pounded out his column. Sometimes he stayed at home and had what he called "a day of genius," during which he would call Noël Coward in London, Miriam Hopkins and three or four other stars on the West coast, order flowers sent by telegram to friends all over the world, and in other glamorous ways manage to spend a couple of thousand dollars. He once sent Dorothy Hall, for her opening in the Preston Sturges play, *Child of Manhattan*, four hundred dollars' worth of orchids! When I took mild exception to this particular extravagance, he phoned down to the florist in the lobby of the Essex House and had them send up to me every single flower in the place.

"There," Ward said as they arrived by the bucketful, "that ought to satisfy you." And I had come home on the bus to save taxi fare! Of course I never let him know about this or my other economies as they only would have confirmed his opinion of me as a little girl who just never would catch on to big city ways. The fact that Miriam Hopkins always referred to me as "Little Joan"—she only started to call me Jean a few years ago—did not help matters any for me either.

Ward had, and has, the saving grace of humor, and virtually everything he did or said amused me. Some days I would come home from the office and find him entertaining not only, say, Tallulah Bankhead, Gertrude Lawrence and Leland Hayward but "a bevy of beauties," as Ward put it, unknown to me and even sometimes to Ward. This caused me considerable consternation only because it upset Pinkey, who had moved up from the Fifty Third street apartment and was now bartender at apartment 3802.

"Miss Jean," she would say, "that girl in the pink dress has two pairs of your stockings and a bottle of your perfume in her handbag." Or, "That pretty dark one over there took all of your lace handkerchiefs."

I would say, aghast, "You mean, stole them?"

She would sigh. "I don't think you can call it that because Mr. Ward told them to help themselves."

Several times Ward complained that he couldn't work in 3802, so I took an unfurnished apartment down on the ninth floor of the Essex House—apartment 9B it was—and had a fine time fixing it up with furniture from John Golden's storehouse at Fort Lee. The living-room rug was the one from the play *Salt*."

Appendix D

Chicago Newspaperman Joe Hyams Goes Hollywood

Journalist Joe Hyams, who was sent by the *New York Herald Tribune* to do a story on illegal immigration coming across the California border, became a devoted Beverly Hills Hotel devotee.

Joe Hyams, who died in 2008, was the author of bestselling biographies of Hollywood stars. Hyams was born in Cambridge, Massachusetts. While attending Harvard University, he enlisted in the U.S. Army in 1942. He received a Purple Heart and was awarded the Bronze Star Medal while serving in the South Pacific. He later covered the war for *Stars and Stripes*, the official newspaper of the United States Armed Forces. He earned bachelors and masters degrees at New York University, after returning from military service.

In 1951, the *New York Herald Tribune* sent him to do an article on illegal immigration to the United States, according to Wikipedia. "He was flown to Mexico on a small airplane and came back into the United States with a group crossing the border illegally. Once the story was complete, his editor told him that a room was waiting for him at the Beverly Hills Hotel. 'Take a break, and if you get a chance to interview any movie stars, go for it.' Asked by a man seated at the hotel's pool what he was doing at the hotel, he replied that he was supposed to interview movie stars. 'How would you like to interview Humphrey Bogart?' was the reply from what turned out to be Bogart's press agent. When Hyams arrived, Bogart was behind the bar and offered him a drink. Hyams asked for a Coke and Bogart reacted angrily: 'I don't trust any bastard who doesn't drink, especially a pipe-smoking newspaperman...or a man who has more hair than I have.' At this, Hyams pocketed his notebook and headed for the door. 'I don't drink,' he said on his way out, 'and I certainly have more hair on my head than you do.' Bogart liked the courage of the reply and not only granted Hyams an interview, but as soon as it appeared invited him to lunch. In addition to the interview with Humphrey Bogart, within the week Hyams had interviewed Lauren Bacall, Katharine Hepburn, Frank Sinatra and Spencer Tracy. The *Herald Tribune* had him relocated to Los Angeles. He covered Hollywood as a syndicated columnist from 1951 to 1964.

"After leaving the *Herald Tribune,* Hyams covered Hollywood for the *Saturday Evening Post, Ladies' Home Journal, Redbook* and other publications.

"He was the author, or co-author, of more than two-dozen books, most of which were biographies of the celebrities he covered, including *Bogie* in 1966, *Bogart & Bacall: A Love Story* in 1975 and *James Dean: Little Boy Lost* in 1992. He co-authored celebrity autobiographies, with Chuck Norris on *The Secret of Inner Strength: My Story* and worked on *Michael Reagan: On the Outside Looking In*, with the adopted son of the former President. His own autobiography, *Mislaid in Hollywood,* was written in 1973. He also wrote novels set in Hollywood, such as *The Pool* and *Murder at the Academy Awards.*

"His 1979 book *Zen in the Martial Arts* was built on his many years of studying martial arts with such figures as Bong Soo Han, Bruce Lee, and Ed Parker. He first became involved in the martial arts during his wartime service in the U.S. Army, when he was regularly beaten up for being Jewish. After the war he became a student of kenpo karate and studied Jeet Kune Do with Bruce Lee, as well as becoming proficient in eight other martial arts disciplines. Melissa Hyams said the slim book 'isn't really about martial arts. It's about life and philosophy, and how to turn a negative into a positive, how to defuse a situation by the way you handle it. That's what he'll most be remembered for.' With penologist Tom Murton, he wrote *Accomplices to the Crime: The Arkansas Prison Scandal,* a 1969 nonfiction account that was the basis for the 1980 film *Brubaker* starring Robert Redford. In 1991 he wrote the non-fiction work *Flight of the Avenger: George Bush at War."*

His second marriage was to 24-year-old actress Elke Sommer in November 1964 in a civil ceremony in Nevada.

My father interviewed Sommer for the General Features Syndicate in 1963.

Elke Sommer presents a sizzling image on the screen and she is just as beautiful and appealing in the harsh light of day. Looking at her (if you should be that lucky), you would never guess that she was once a milkmaid. Or that she dreamed of owning a farm.

"I was 14 when my father died," she said, "and my mother and I went to live in a village near Nuremberg. We had only $70 a month to live on, so I got up early every morning and milked cows to earn a few extra pennies. The big thing I wanted was a farm, because I love animals. We lived in two small

Appendix D

rooms, but I had two dogs, a porcupine that would crawl into the wool basket, a hedgehog, a cat and some birds.

"My father was a Protestant minister—there have been ministers in his family for generations. My mother's people were all schoolteachers and professors. I go to church, to the Lutheran church, when I feel I need it."

There was a table-to-table buzz when Elke walked into the Café Pierre in a figure-hugging white dress, which was not surprising as she is about the closest thing to Marilyn Monroe to come along. Elke is taller—about five feet six—but her eyes are blue like Marilyn's and she has the same skin impact and almost platinum hair.

"Marilyn was the one screen star I wanted to meet in America," she said. "But she died before I got here."

Elke was born in Berlin and she was a European film star before she made her English-language film debut in "Don't Bother to Knock." She speaks German, French, Italian, Spanish and English. Her new picture will be "The Art of Love," a comedy co-starring James Garner, which Universal will release in June

In the spring of 1964 Elke got word that she was to be interviewed by Joe Hyams, who wrote about Hollywood people and high-jinks for the *New York Herald Tribune*. His piece on Elke was for the *Saturday Evening Post* and she recalls that he arrived "all prepared and cynical." The *Post* said he spent several weeks interviewing Elke, which was right away a tip-off that he enjoyed the work.

"She sleeps in the nude, her left thumb in her mouth, her right arm cuddling a stuffed lamb," Hyams wrote. "Asleep, she resembles a child. But awake and in fluid motion before the cameras, she makes Bardot look like an awkward schoolgirl. There are critics who deride her talent, but her movies have earned her a half dozen fur coats and three homes. She says she has no time for love, but the European press claims that two men have committed suicide over her...In Europe her first name suffices—like Gina, Sophia, Brigitte or Liz."

Appendix E

Valentino Writes

The following archival news article was pulled from ClassicGlamourChic, and written by none other than the Sheik himself, Rudolph Valentino! (Or, more likely, some anonymous press agent sweating in the Hollywood publicity backrooms.)

This is going to be in the nature of a confession. I live, perhaps not a Jekyll and Hyde life, but at least a dual life. There are two Rudolph Valentinos.

There is the one that you see on the screen, and there is the one that you seldom see at all.

One is a romantic fellow who swaggers through life, makes love with great ardor, fights and wins battles against great odds and in the end clasps his sweetheart to his arms, or else dies heroically to atone for his misdeeds.

The other—and the real one—is a hard-working young man who has had more than his share of hardship, and is now enjoying more than his share of good fortune.

I am not just being modest when I say that it is the former in which the public is interested. The popular conception of Valentino is a blend of *Julio* of "The Four Horsemen," *Monsieur Beaucaire*, and the *Sheik* himself. I am glad that the interesting qualities of these young men do attach to me in the public mind, for otherwise my lot might be decidedly different. And because I realize that my shadow self is the more interesting, I am in no danger of outgrowing the size of my hat. For the same reason, I don't like to make personal appearances. The fans don't want to see Rudolph; they want to see *Julio*. I don't want to disappoint them.

The position of a motion-picture star is unique, and seemingly interesting to other persons besides himself. The widespread distribution of films brings him to the attention of the whole world. No other medium has ever reached so many people. He appears simultaneously in New York, Paris, Painted Post, and Singapore. Also, there seems to be more glamour about picture players than about the stars of the stage. I think this is due to the fact that the films leave more to the imagination regarding the personality of the performer. When you see an actor on the stage, you see him more completely. You know how he talks and how he looks in the flesh. By this complete survey you may be convinced that the actor or actress is a superior human, yet you are conscious all the time that he or she is only human.

But you don't get so close to the picture actor. There is something eerie in the fact that this person appears before you only in disembodied form. There is a chance for the imagination to paint around the personality of this once-removed hero a picture of perfection hues. Distance lends enchantment to the view. Ask my valet what kind of a man this Valentino is, and if he does not give you a discouraging picture, I have mistaken the quality of his intelligence.

Being a motion-picture star has its disadvantages. He cannot go to public places conveniently and comfortably. When he goes to the theaters he must wait until after the play has started and then slip into a back seat. He cannot make an appointment to meet any one in a hotel lobby, for if he does he soon will have a crowd around him. When he walks on the street people turn and stare, and some even follow. For the sake of my professional standing, I hope this will always be true in my own case. But I am sure you will agree with me that living in a show case has its disadvantages. Don't think for a minute that I don't appreciate the attention. Without it, I would be very unhappy, for I would know that I was no longer of interest to the jury that makes us or breaks us—the public.

Here is a problem which always seems like a new one to me. If I go to a place where a crowd has gathered, how shall I greet them? If I bow and smile, I know that some will say: "Well, isn't he the vain young man to think that we have been waiting here to see him?"

If I walk up casually with the thought—and I frequently have it—that it is foolish for so many people to come out to get a look at me, I fear that I am courting this remark: "Up-stage, isn't he? Too good to speak to us."

If anybody can ease my mind as to the attitude in such a situation I shall be greatly indebted to him. If you are ever in a crowd [as I] am, you will know what is going on in my [mind.] Please have a little sympathy for my perplexity and please know that I do appreciate your coming, for acclaim is the food which feeds the actor's soul. If you and others like you were not interested in seeing me, I should have to stop acting and take up some other occupation. This might bring ...thousands, but, oh, the difference to me!

The editor of this magazine, in asking me to write this article, stated in a letter:

'You are a star who, after luck gave you your chance in "The Four Horsemen," succeeded notably because of your good looks. This physical appearance has appealed generally, but accentedly to women. As a consequence you have been pitchforked into a position, whether or not it has been one of your own seeking, which has made you famous for one thing. No matter what good work you do, how distinguished your acting may be, the fact remains that the name Valentino has become a household word for an attractive male.'

'Write, if you will, an article revealing the state of mind of a man such as I have described. What are his sensations as he moves from place to place? What part of this enforced experience is boring and what part of it is stimulating? What type of conduct is imposed on him willy nilly?'

Those are the questions I am trying to answer. Some of them I have already touched on. One phase of this is particularly embarrassing for me to discuss—the "attractive male" part.

Now, every man wants to be attractive to women, for love is the dominant note in life, and a man's happiness depends more upon his finding and winning the woman who will complement his life than any other factor. His ability to do this depends to great extent on his attractiveness, yet a man feels a bit sheepish when his own personality is up for discussion. I confess that I share this confusion, and I repeat that I realize that people know my screen prototype rather than myself.

"No matter what good work he does—"... Well, that is discouraging. I am speaking frankly and seriously. Ever since Harry Leon Wilson wrote "Merton of the Movies" it has become impossible for a picture star to speak seriously without feeling self-conscious, but I shall do it anyhow. Like *Merton* I want to be a good actor and I want to be known as a good actor. I should rather be so considered than to have any other honor. Acting is my profession and I take the same pride in that the painter, the novelist, the lawyer take in theirs.

I am not so modest or so unbusinesslike that I do not want to be thought of as an "attractive male." This is based on two reasons. One is that every man likes to be thought of as something of a dashing fellow, and the second is that otherwise my productions would drop off in public demand. Motion-picture fans are more interested in personalities than high art. I can almost hear a chorus chanting, "You should be thankful of that." To which I reply that I am. But still I would like to be thought of sometimes as a man doing good work.

To be called "The Sheik," a term applied to me because of a picture by that name in which I played the title rôle, is, I must say, annoying. In the first place, I think my own work in the picture was bad. In the second place, I am not a sheik in the sense that the word is used. One of my brutal friends tells me that I am merely posing when I say I don't like the designation. Well, that is a problem for the psychoanalysts and too deep for me.

Having arrived at the position of stardom, I feel a desire to remain there. This imposes upon me a regimen of living far more rigorous, I believe, than is imposed on the average successful business man.

While working on a picture I arise at five o'clock in the morning and am at my studio riding ring by six. I ride horseback for an hour under the tutelage of Mario Carillo, a former captain of Italian cavalry, who is putting me through the same course as though I were in training to become an army officer.

Then I don my costume and make-up and am ready for work at eight thirty.

Acting before the camera, and attention to the hundreds of details which attend picture making, take up my day. I seldom leave the studio before seven at night. You will believe me when I say that I am in bed at nine. On the evening before a recent holiday, I planned to celebrate by going to the theater. After dinner I was so sleepy that I decided to forgo even that mild dissipation. ...

In connection with the conduct imposed upon a star I might add that it is easier to become a star than it is to remain one. Once the [spot]light begins to play upon the actor, he is like a specimen under a microscope. Under the magnifying glass his wings frequently look singed and sometimes they are not visible at all.

This spotlight follows him after he leaves the studio wherever he may go. If he should arise late some morning and neglect to shave—this has no reference to my own recent beard—the report is circulated that So-and-so, always so immaculate on the screen, is really unkempt in private life.

If he mistreats his wife, he is a brute, and should not be allowed on the screen. If he loves her, he is supposed to sacrifice some of his romantic appeal to the feminine theater patrons.

If he appears at a café with a jolly crowd, he is dissipating terribly.

I was invited attend a New Year's Eve party at a public place. It was to be a perfectly respectable celebration such as were attended by good people all over this country, which does not mean, however, that all of the eighteen amendments would be kept absolutely inviolate. I had heard reports that the dry law enforcement agents would be unusually active, so I stayed at home, for I knew that if any liquor were found on any one at my table, headlines from coast to coast would read:

Appendix E 187

Valentino Caught in Liquor Raid

The only place I can find any privacy is in my own home, so for that reason I stay there most of the time that I am not in the studio.

But if the star's private life is an open book to the public, his professional life is even more so. He is held responsible for many things.

If the story is bad, the star is blamed. He didn't write it, but the public reasons that he should know better than to appear in bad stories. In many cases the star has no say in the matter, but must appear in the stories assigned to him. This does not apply, however, to such players as Norma Talmadge, Doulas Fairbanks, Mary Pickford, and Charles Chaplin, who produce their own pictures and therefore have complete authority.

If the direction is bad, the star is blamed. It is almost an impossible matter for the spectator to decide whether excellence or failure on the part of the actor to make a scene effective is due to the player or the director, but the latter is so remote a figure that the public points its finger of scorn at the person it can see.

By the same token, I suppose that good work on the part of the author or director reflects credit on the star and that he receives praise which he does not deserve. But the slings and arrows of criticism seem to strike the cuticle harder than the roses of applause.

So the star finds himself the focusing point of both the camera and the picturegoers. If he steps to one side, or is too forward or too backward, he gets out of focus. So he must keep in the one position. But even so, if he remains there long enough, he will find the spotlight wavering and seeking other targets. That spotlight is a fickle jade. There are fixed stars in the firmament but none in the motion-picture skies. All of my energies will be devoted to keeping such position as I have attained, and I want to remain in pictures as long as I can, for if ever a man enjoyed his work, that man is myself.

Appendix F

Damon Runyon Marvels at the Millennium Biltmore's own "Guys and Dolls"

"You can stagger from actor to actor in the lobby of the Biltmore at almost any time of the day or night."—Newspaper columnist, short story writer Damon Runyon.

"While strolling along the Rialto in Los Angeles the other day in my spats I was struck by a thought," Runyon, perhaps the most famous journalist in history after Walter Winchell, wrote in one of his columns. "I wore these spats through a special act of the Los Angeles City Council. It is against the local ordinances for a man to wear spats in Los Angeles, but I was permitted to wear 'em when I explained that I was not allowed to wear 'em at home." Runyon is perhaps most famous for his fictional characters who were in the Broadway musical, *Guys and Dolls*.

"Anyway, I was struck by a thought, as follows, to wit:

"In New York you never see anybody you know. In Los Angeles you know everybody you see. At least you know who they are, which amounts to the same thing. This is one of the advantages of a well-regulated Rialto.

"In New York I would never see an actor or theatrical celebrity of any kind at large, except on the stage, or in a club. Nowadays they live out on Long Island or hide away in cavernous apartment houses far uptown, and it is difficult to find them without a search warrant.

"In Los Angeles they are all over the place. You can stagger from actor to actor in the lobby of the Biltmore at almost any time of the day or night. ...

"Mr. Harry Ruby and Mr. Bert Kalmar, who wrote popular songs and musical scores, and what-not, and are famed all through the Roaring Forties as extemporaneous entertainers of great cunning, were reclining side by side on one of the good Mr. Charley Baad's settees.

"They came to Los Angeles to write 'The Love Call,' and are remaining to write other things. They wanted to know if I had seen Paul Gerard Smith, the playwright, who had just passed through the lobby, and who is out here working as a gag man for Buster Keaton."

A museum in and of itself, the Millennium Biltmore occasionally put out the red carpet for traveling treasure shows. An amulet, a religious token formed of genuine amber with a sacred beetle imprisoned in the center was in one show.

"The tiny amulet, less than half an inch long and weighing a fraction of an ounce, is said to be invested with incalculable powers in the minds of the inhabitants of the Zaidam Swamp region in eastern Turkestan near the Kwenlun mountains," the *Los Angeles Times* said.

"According to its present owner, it was obtained by her via the 'grapevine' route from an aged 'desert rat' in the Gobi desert. Were its presence in the hands of a Christian known while the young lady was still in China, it would have precipitated embarrassing circumstances. Miss Layne said the piece of amber is considered particularly sacred by the adherents of that religion because the amber imprisons a sacred beetle which is held in reverence almost as highly as the statues of Buddha. Its enclosure in the amber is said to be extremely rare, Miss Layne said 'and is construed by the inhabitants of that far away district as a sign of the gods.' The amulet is said to be worth several hundred dollars."

In a switch from mysticism to more heavenly matters, Millennium Biltmore Assistant Manager Sid Sterling was once appointed official "Bible sleuth" of the Los Angeles hotel fraternity.

It appears that a Bible "crime wave" was running rampant for a time.

Bibles were disappearing from the Millennium Biltmore and other hotels in droves. This came to the attention of A.B.T. Moore of Washington, secretary of the Gideon Bible Association. Moore decided that this wholesale pilfering of bibles had to be stopped, so he has appointed representatives in the different hotels to keep an eye on Gideon snatchers.

"It takes a particularly mean person to steal a Bible," noted Sterling. Not long after Nobel Prize winning novelist Sinclair Lewis was photographed reading a Gideon without anyone even slightly hinting that the author of *Arrowsmith* and *Elmer Gantry* had any intention of taking it home. It should be noted that The Gideon Society wants you to keep a Bible, but not by the dozen as happened in L.A.

In another syndicated "Damon Runyon Says" column the famous columnist noted that, "It is almost with a sense of guilt that your correspondent again mentions the weather, in view of the fact that these lines will be read by subscribers huddled over leaky steam radiators in the far frozen East, but it is really a matter of sartorial news that gentlemen are walking about the streets of Los Angeles in their shirt sleeves.

"I am informed that it is a winter fashion that prevails here due to the exigencies of sunshine in these parts. It is rapidly gaining ground among the elite, but it is what you might call a tough break for the famous golfers of the land who are falling off every incoming train for the two big golf tournaments that start here presently—the $2500 Long Beach championship and the $10,000 Los Angeles open. These famous golfers are arriving here equipped with the very latest in golf gaberdines. They are coming in coats, blazers, surtouts, jackets and what-not, prepared to astonish the natives with their sartorial glory when they tee off. They will be greatly disappointed when they discover that coats are not only out of style, but really quite uncomfortable.

"The only citizen of Los Angeles who habitually wears a coat at this season of the year is Mr. Dick Scollin, one of the assistant managers of the Hotel Biltmore. Mr. Scollin wears a morning coat, with long spiked tails. I am informed that there is something in the city ordinances of Los Angeles that requires Mr. Scollin to wear this coat, that strangers to the city may know that coats are not unknown in Southern California and that everybody could wear them if they desired. At certain intervals during the day Mr. Scollin is permitted to repair to the park across the way from the Biltmore, hang his coat on the limb of a palm tree and sit in the shade until he cools off. Then he must resume the coat and return to the Biltmore and exhibit himself to the traveling public.

"Mr. Scollin was the only man who knew what ailed Mr. Warren W. Brown of Chicago when Mr. Brown collapsed weakly in a lily bed in the lobby of the Biltmore today. Mr. Brown is one of my most distinguished contemporaries in the matter of reporting the Alabama-Washington football game, the big golf tournament and the many other sports events that impend hereabouts.

"He came in from a brisk walk along Olive street and suddenly tumbled over among the lilies. A crowd quickly gathered, including Mr. Benny Leonard, the retired but not so very retiring light-weight champion of the world; Mr. Spike Robinson, the local boulevardier; Mr. Joe Benjamin, representing the manly art of scrambling ears, Mr. Floyd Fitzsimmons, the celebrated promoter and other prominent natives and visiting firemen. They stood about undecided what to do about Mr. Brown's collapse until Mr. Scollin rushed forward, with his spiked tails flapping furiously. He took one look at Mr. Brown, then motioned the lads to enter a huddle formation while he got out his pocket knife.

"It developed that all that was the matter with Mr. Brown was that he still had on fleece-lined underwear, with which he repels the rigors of the breezes off Lake Michigan. It seems that he had had this underwear sewed on in the early fall, not expecting he would have to remove it until the next grass. Long experience with thoughtless visitors from the frigid zones has taught Mr. Scollin that the only thing necessary is to cut the patient out of his fleece lining. Mr. Brown quickly recovered, but had a slight relapse when Mr. Pat Shanley of the famous hotel firm of Shanley and Furniss appeared in one of his characteristic makeups. I would not attempt here to describe even one of Mr. Shanley's makeups, because my readers might think I am seeing things."

www.ingramcontent.com/pod-product-compliance
Lightning Source LLC
Chambersburg PA
CBHW051928160426
43198CB00012B/2076